TALKING AND LISTENING TOGETHER

COUPLE COMMUNICATION I

Sherod Miller, Ph. D.

Phyllis A. Miller, Ph. D.

Elam W. Nunnally, Ph. D.

Daniel B. Wackman, Ph. D.

Printed in the United States of America

Sixth Printing: March 1995

Illustrated by Barrie Maguire

**INTERPERSONAL
COMMUNICATION
PROGRAMS, INC.**

**7201 South Broadway
Littleton, Colo. 80122
Phone (303) 794-1764**

FOREWORD

Background of Couple Communication

The roots of Couple Communication extend back to the late 1960's at the University of Minnesota Family Study Center. There, blessed with an outstanding faculty and a substantial research grant from the National Institute of Mental Health, authors Sherod Miller, Elam Nunnally, and Daniel Wackman met and became a research and program-development team.

Their initial research focused on the transition from engagement to early marriage and on the conditions that supported couples in making the transition successfully. The research confirmed that effective communication was central to the change process. The team also identified specific communication concepts and skills, which they taught to couples to improve the partners' abilities to discuss day-to-day concerns in a productive manner.

Recognizing that relationships, in addition to having been initiated, were also maintained, strengthened, and destroyed through communication, the team broadened the spectrum of couples in their program. They began to include partners in all stages who wished to learn communication skills.

Over the years, many investigators have continued to study Couple Communication. According to Dr. Karen Wampler at the Texas Tech University, Department of Human Development and Family Studies,

"Couple Communication is the most extensively documented intervention program ever developed." Since 1971, thirty-one studies have been published in professional journals or as doctoral dissertations. More are in progress. Most of the research has been conducted at major universities throughout the U.S., in cooperation with Couple Communication instructors in a variety of community contexts. In a nutshell, the findings show:

- Very positive impact on communication following the program
- Increases in relationship satisfaction

Couples in the studies have ranged widely. Partners have included those in various economic groups, older and younger people, as well as troubled and well-functioning partnerships. In short, partners who take Couple Communication complete the program, gain positive results, and enjoy it.

The Couple Communication program has reached far beyond its research base. To date, more than 200,000 couples have participated in Couple Communication throughout the United States, as well as in Canada, Europe, Australia, New Zealand, and Japan. The program has been translated into several languages.

The instructors of Couple Communication come from a number of backgrounds. Most are human service professionals — therapists, counselors, ministers, and teachers. Others are lay couples who have benefitted from participating in a Couple Communication group and who have taken Instructor Training to teach the program.

Over time, the research and the practical experiences of the instructors and participant couples have provided new information about teaching communication skills to partners. This revision of the program draws extensively on the learnings from these formal and informal sources. To help in the further development of Couple Communication reflected in this book, Phyllis Miller has joined the three original authors.

Couple Communication Materials

Instructors see that each couple who participates in the program receives their own Couple Packet. The Couple Packet contains materials for learning during the sessions, for practice between sessions, and for continued application after the program. Each Couple Packet includes two of these workbooks, one Awareness Wheel skills mat, one Listening Cycle skills mat, and two sets of pocket cards.

Features of Couple Communication

Several features make Couple Communication a leader among skill-learning programs. The program gives you:

- *Conceptual maps for increasing awareness* of yourself and your partner, and of how the two of you communicate together

- *Eleven specific talking and listening skills* for sending and receiving messages more clearly and accurately

- An emphasis on both *attitudinal and behavioral* aspects of conflict resolution and relationship building

- *Accelerated skill-learning technology (skills mats)* to help you transfer the Couple Communication concepts and skills into your everyday lives

- *Communication exercises to apply the skills with children* for enriching your family communication

- *The most extensively researched communication skills program* available for couples

Benefits of Couple Communication

Partners who have participated in Couple Communication report a wide range of benefits from the program, including:

- More effective ways of talking and listening

- Better understanding of self and partner

- Higher self-worth

- Faster, better resolutions of conflict

- More enjoyment of one another

- New ways of being intimate

- Improved parent-child communication

- More productive communication at work

You and your partner can experience these benefits, too, by learning and using the concepts and skills presented in this book. Welcome to Couple Communication.

ACKNOWLEDGMENTS

A large network of people have been involved in the growth of Couple Communication I for more than two decades. With deep appreciation we list the names of our mentors and colleagues who have made substantial contributions:

Reuben Hill, Earl Beatt, Virginia Satir, William Fawcett Hill, Sidney Jourard, Eeva Nunnally, Kathy Wackman, Ramon Corrales, Chet Evenson, Jim Maddock, Karen Wampler, Bob Friederichsen, Ray Becker, David and Karen Olson, David and Vera Mace, Michael Paula, Liisa Tuovinen, Kay and Ted Packard, Tres and Loras Goddard, Bob and Renee Noles, Paul Giblin, William Hudson, Zellie Earnest, Julie McDonnell, Gary Oliver, Bob Bolenbaucher, and the Staffs at Minneapolis Family Service and Denver-Area Kaiser Permanente.

Equally important are the Couple Communication Instructors and Training Associates who have worked so well with over 200,000 couples.

Lastly, we want to thank the many couples who have written to tell us about their experiences in Couple Communication and about the impact it has had on their lives.

CONTENTS

Introduction

While growing up, if you lived with both of your parents, you probably saw them face conflict and make many decisions. Perhaps you observed them decide how much money to spend on a certain item, what to do on a particular evening, or simply, who should put the dog out. The odds are high, however, that you never watched your parents work through a serious difference skillfully and respectfully, let alone constructively discuss their own patterns of decision making or conflict resolution.

In times past, gender and position usually prescribed decision making and conflict resolving at home and work. Seldom did partners openly talk about their communication processes — how they listened, talked, and related. However, in today's fast-paced, complex, and uncertain world of opportunities, most of us realize another way is possible.

Talking and Listening Together presents communication concepts and skills to increase your interpersonal competence and to help you and your partner live more satisfactory and meaningful lives together.

CARING AND COMMUNICATION

In any communicating you do, every message you send contains two component parts: attitude and behavior. *Attitudes derive from the combined beliefs, feelings, and intentions you hold. Behaviors — the verbal and nonverbal actions you take — reflect and stem from your underlying attitudes.* So, each exchange you make with your partner reflects your underlying attitude about yourself and about your partner.

Two basic attitudes you can hold toward yourself are:

- I Don't Care About Me

- I Care About Me

In every situation you communicate either that you do not value, respect, and count yourself — you do not care — or that you do.

Likewise, two corresponding attitudes you can hold toward your partner are:

- I Don't Care About You

- I Care About You

Again, in any exchange, you communicate either that you do not value, respect, and count your partner — you do not care — or that you do.

Behavior Reflects Attitude

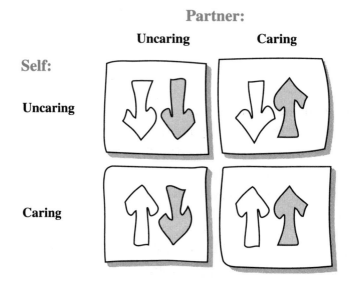

The uncaring or caring attitudes you hold about yourself and your partner express your momentary or long-term assumptions about one another's significance. These underlying opinions about your own worth and your partner's worth form a foundation for your relationship, which in turn impacts your own and your partner's communication.

All four self-partner attitudinal postures begin with the pronoun "I," illustrating an important assumption in Couple Communication: *Each partner develops his or her own attitudes and is responsible for his or her own behavior. In other words, "I" choose either not to care or to care.*

Why Learn Communication Skills?

Partners have been communicating for thousands of years with a caring spirit. No substitute exists for love and caring in communication! However, even with a genuine caring attitude, communication can be unclear, inept, or misunderstood. This is where skill enters.

Over the past thirty years, behavioral scientists have carefully studied the *process* of human communication and have discovered that *certain behaviors yield more predictable outcomes.* Specific behavioral skills and processes enable people to send messages more accurately, effectively, and efficiently. Furthermore, studies indicate that couples who learn how to resolve their conflicts and differences effectively and efficiently stay together more frequently than couples who do not possess this interpersonal competence.

No Skill and Misuse of Skills

An uncaring attitude and no skill, combined in a relationship, make for difficult living. Verbal, if not physical, abuse often goes with such a relationship. But rarely do partners lack some portion of a caring attitude. Communication skills can help express and demonstrate caring attitudes more clearly.

Without a caring attitude, unfortunately, learning and using Couple Communication skills can turn you into a more sophisticated manipulator. And if your partner discounts himself or herself and allows your manipulative behavior to continue, your relationship will suffer. Either uncaring attitude or lack of skill can retard or destroy a relationship.

However, by combining a caring attitude and skill in communication, you can build self-esteem and other-esteem, and strengthen your relationship. *Caring, skilled communication processes yield the most satisfying and effective outcomes between partners.*

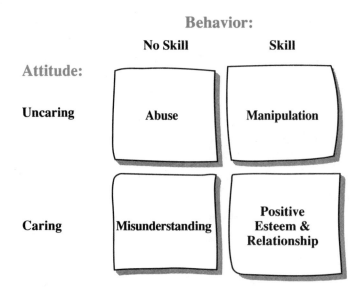

The Main Goal of Couple Communication

The main goal, the watermark, of Couple Communication is to help you and your partner skillfully communicate *I-care-about-me and I-care-about-you* attitudes around your day-to-day issues.

Each chapter in *Talking and Listening Together* takes an element of a caring attitude and shows you maps and skills for effectively expressing the caring in behavior.

MORE ABOUT COMMUNICATION

You may wish sometimes that you and your partner could have more time to be together and to talk. Often though, in this fast-paced age, time can be hard to find. However, when the two of you are together, it is not just how much time you spend talking that counts; rather, it is *what* you talk about and *how* you talk and listen to each other that matters.

The *What* of Your Conversation

The *what* of your communication — the specific things you converse about with your partner — depends on a host of factors, for example: your interests, experiences, and values; your point in the life cycle; your occupation; and your family make-up. In addition, various external circumstances, such as current events or even time of day influence the content of your conversation. Four directions in which you may focus your conversation include external topics, yourself, your partner, or your relationship.

Topic-messages focus on things, events, ideas, places, or on people who are not present and participating in the conversation:

"Carol has soccer practice tonight."

"Is there gas in the car?"

Self-messages focus on you as a person — your experiences, thoughts, feelings, wants, and actions:

"I've been feeling great lately."

"I'm not sure what I want to do."

Partner-messages focus on your partner as a person — his or her experiences, thoughts, feelings, and actions:

"You really seem disturbed about that."

"Do you expect to finish today?"

Both self-messages and partner-messages focus on a single person, either you or your partner. In this sense, their focus is *personal,* expressing more personal involvement than topic messages do.

Relationship-messages, the fourth kind of focus, also contain much personal involvement:

"I feel pleased when you listen to me closely."

"I will back you up if you want to change careers."

Relationship-messages are about *you and me together* — our joint experience, impact on one another, and various aspects of our relationship. The messages are usually more intimate than either self-messages or partner-messages.

Some people talk primarily about topics and seldom disclose anything about themselves personally. Other people focus on themselves and show little interest in the experiences or concerns of those around them. Still others readily focus on others present and encourage them to talk about themselves. The least frequently focused-upon messages are the relationship messages. People have greater tendency to talk about "it," "you," or "me" than about "you and me — us."

Pause for a moment and think about the focus of your own conversations. What (who) do you spend most of your time talking about? Is there a balance? Do you spend too little or too much time talking about yourself? How much do you tune into others? How often do you make relationship statements?

Distinguishing among topic-, self-, other-, and relationship-messages allows you more awareness and choice in your conversations.

Issues

Recognizing the differences among content messages also provides a context for understanding the types of issues you encounter, individually and together with your partner.

An issue is anything (situation, event, experience, awareness) that concerns or is important to you or your partner. Issues get your attention. Some of the issues most partnerships face at one time or another fall under the three categories — topical, personal, and relational.

While issues do have a primary focus — topical, personal, or relational — they are not always this neatly packaged. Often the focus is mixed. For example, career (topical) involves togetherness/apartness (relational), or faith (personal) is influenced by similarity/difference (relational). Sometimes couples play out conflicts at the topical or personal level which are really unrecognized or unresolved relationship issues. Knowing the differences among types of issues can help you identify and deal with your issues more effectively.

All individuals and couples have issues. These attention-getters arise out of normal, everyday situations and vary according to your stage in life. Some issues are viewed as positive, others as negative. They crop up when circumstances change, for example, when you have a baby, change jobs, or move from one place to another. They arise when you or your partner feel some dissatisfaction or want change. They occur when something unexpected happens. Issues also surface when you and your partner anticipate the future.

TYPES OF ISSUES

Topical

housing	exercise	leisure
education	drugs/alcohol	pets
work	parents	chores
children	career	moving
friends	time	projects
money	in-laws	clothes
food	transportation	travel

Personal (Self or Partner)

self-esteem	productivity	goals
identity	appearance	success
energy	responsibility	failure
values	expectations	attitude
freedom	faith	habits
discipline	recognition	skills
health	creativity	death

Relational (You and Me, Us)

togetherness/apartness	celebration
closeness/distance	trust
equality/subordination	affection
stability/change	commitment
agreement/disagreement	sex
similarity/difference	acceptance
inclusion/exclusion	expectations
conflict/harmony	boundaries
collaboration/competition	appreciation
support/control	communication
understanding/misunderstanding	

Issues require varying amounts of mental, emotional, and physical energy. *The process of dealing with issues usually involves making decisions and sometimes resolving conflicts.*

If handled well, issues may bring personal and relationship growth. Your confidence and ability to deal with issues successfully will increase as you develop more effective ways to discuss them.

The *How* of Your Conversation

What you and your partner talk about is important. But more important for determining the quality of your relationship is *how* the two of you converse. This book teaches you *how* to talk about and listen to the *what*.

A BRIEF OVERVIEW OF THE BOOK

Talking and Listening Together is divided into four chapters, each presenting a framework and skills related to an important aspect of interpersonal communication. Each chapter also includes exercises to give you practice using the frameworks and skills with your current issues. As you progress from chapter to chapter, the frameworks and skills build upon each other, providing an integrated approach for improving your communication with your partner.

Chapter 1: Caring About Yourself introduces the Awareness Wheel, a map for helping you *recognize and expand* your self-awareness surrounding issues. You will also learn six related talking skills for *expressing* your awareness more completely and accurately.

Chapter 2: Caring About Your Partner teaches five simple, but powerful listening skills for tuning into your partner's awareness. You will also learn the Listening Cycle — an approach for ensuring complete and accurate understanding.

Chapter 3: Resolving Conflicts: Mapping Issues helps you identify your typical decision-making, conflict-resolving patterns for issues. It also integrates the talking and listening skills (from Chapters 1 and 2) into a practical, collaborative decision-making, conflict-resolving process, called Mapping an Issue.

Chapter 4: Choosing Communication Styles: Ways of Talking and Listening describes the characteristics of four distinct styles of talking and listening, as well as the positive and negative impacts of the styles on conversations with your partner. The chapter provides an integrated summary and perspective of all the concepts and skills taught in Couple Communication I.

Chapter Worksheets

Worksheets/exercises related to the Couple Communication program are included at the end of each chapter. Some are for use in the structured program and others are for practice and application on your own.

Pre- and Post-Questionnaires

The questionnaires are designed to help you to set goals and evaluate your progress. The questions in each relate to the concepts and skills taught in *Talking and Listening Together*. Take some time before and after reading the book or participating in a structured course to answer the questions.

How to Use the Book

If you participate in Couple Communication I, your instructor will give you directions for using the book. If you are reading *Talking and Listening Together* on your own, we suggest that you read one chapter at a time, and complete two or three exercises before continuing. This provides an opportunity to practice using concepts and skills from one chapter before learning new material.

PARTICIPATE IN THE COUPLE COMMUNICATION PROGRAM

You can develop your skills more rapidly if you and your partner participate in the Couple Communication program. The course is taught two ways: in a group with other couples and an instructor or as a pair privately with an instructor.

If you do not know a Certified Couple Communication Instructor in your community and would like to participate in a Couple Communication course, contact us. We will be happy to send you the names of Certified Instructors in your state. Write or call us at:

Interpersonal Communication Programs, Inc.
7201 South Broadway
Littleton, Colorado 80122
303-794-1764

PRE-QUESTIONNAIRE

Date _____

Instructions: Before moving into Chapter 1, take this Pre-Questionnaire *to assess* how you currently communicate with your partner, and *to set* your learning goals. The questions relate to the concepts and skills taught in Couple Communication I. Follow the four steps below.

Step 1. Mark each item twice: first with an "X" to represent your *typical* behavior and again with an "O" (circle) to represent your more-so or less-so *desired* behavior. If your *typical* and *desired* behaviors are the same, the "X" and "O" marks will be on the same number. If they are not the same, the marks will fall on different numbers.

When you are with your partner, how often do you:

	Seldom Often	Difference
1. Speak for your partner — put words into his or her mouth?	1 2 3 4 5 6	_____
2. Use your full awareness to reflect on an issue?	1 2 3 4 5 6	_____
3. Share your feelings?	1 2 3 4 5 6	_____
4. Disclose your wants and desires?	1 2 3 4 5 6	_____
5. Listen briefly, then begin talking?	1 2 3 4 5 6	_____
6. Acknowledge what your partner is feeling?	1 2 3 4 5 6	_____
7. Acknowledge your partner's wants and desires?	1 2 3 4 5 6	_____
8. Invite/encourage your partner to expand on his or her point?	1 2 3 4 5 6	_____
9. Ask what he or she is thinking, feeling, and wanting?	1 2 3 4 5 6	_____
10. Summarize your partner's messages to ensure accuracy?	1 2 3 4 5 6	_____
11. Avoid issues?	1 2 3 4 5 6	_____
12. Propose a good time and place to discuss important issues?	1 2 3 4 5 6	_____

	Seldom Often	Difference
13. Force decisions on your partner?	1 2 3 4 5 6	_____
14. Give in to your partner's decisions?	1 2 3 4 5 6	_____
15. Talk about issues but leave them unresolved?	1 2 3 4 5 6	_____
16. Settle issues by compromising — trading something for something?	1 2 3 4 5 6	_____
17. Resolve issues by building agreements collaboratively?	1 2 3 4 5 6	_____
18. Have pleasant, fun conversations?	1 2 3 4 5 6	_____
19. Direct or instruct your partner?	1 2 3 4 5 6	_____
20. Argue and fight?	1 2 3 4 5 6	_____
21. Blame or attack him or her directly?	1 2 3 4 5 6	_____
22. Make spiteful, undercutting remarks indirectly?	1 2 3 4 5 6	_____
23. Explore possible causes of an issue?	1 2 3 4 5 6	_____
24. Brainstorm solutions to an issue?	1 2 3 4 5 6	_____
25. Send clear, complete, and straightforward messages?	1 2 3 4 5 6	_____
Total Difference Score		_____

Step 2. When you have completed marking all the items, calculate the numerical difference between *typical* and *desired* scores for each item and record the results in the "difference" column. If the "X" and "O" are on the same number, the difference = 0. If the "X" is on 5 and the "O" is on 2, the difference = 3. Note that the "O" can be located on a higher or lower number than the "X." Do not be concerned about the higher or lower direction of the scores, just calculate the numerical difference between the marks.

Step 3. Sum the difference scores (for Post-Questionnaire comparison).

Step 4. Look over the Questionnaire above and put a check mark next to each item number (to the left of a question) with a difference score of "2" or more. These relate to skills and processes which would be the most beneficial for you to develop or change. (See the next page to set your learning goals.)

SETTING YOUR LEARNING GOALS

Instructions: From the items you checked on the Pre-Questionnaire (see Step 4 on the previous page), write down five behaviors you want to increase or decrease. Consider these as your major Couple Communication I learning goals.

Goals: **Brief description of behavior to increase or decrease:**

1. Item # _____   _____

2. Item # _____   _____

3. Item # _____   _____

4. Item # _____   _____

5. Item # _____   _____

After you and your partner have each privately completed the Pre-Questionnaire in each of your workbooks, compare your results and share your individual learning goals.

CARING
ABOUT
YOURSELF

dcs

We are the filter through which we communi- cate. What are our experiences, feelings etc.

1

Caring About Yourself

THE AWARENESS WHEEL

The Awareness Wheel is a map to help you become more aware of yourself — what you are experiencing at any point in time. In this chapter, we would like to show you how to use the map to care about yourself better. Once you are familiar with the Awareness Wheel, it can help you understand and care about your partner better, too.

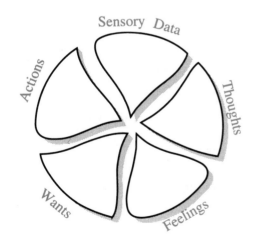

The Awareness Wheel map includes five "zones": sensing, thinking, feeling, wanting, and doing. Each part contains important information about yourself. All five parts are distinct yet interact with each other. All five are ever present in your experience even though you may not be conscious of them. They become available when you tune in to them and use them.

This chapter describes each of the five zones and then shows you how to use the Wheel for:

- Self-Talk — reflecting on issues to understand them and expand your choices

- Communication — disclosing your awareness through specific talking skills

SENSORY DATA — Verbal and Nonverbal Input

Your five senses — sight, sound, smell, taste, and touch — are your immediate points of contact with the outside world. Through these channels, you collect stimuli. In a conversation, sensory data come to you as:

gestures	numbers	stories
tones	words	scent
posture	comments	

The more you pay attention to the subtleties of what you see, hear, smell, taste, and touch, the more you will be aware of what is going on around you. The behaviors of other people, both verbal and nonverbal, become your sensory input — so do time, place, and other contextual cues.

Nonverbal Input

Without ever hearing a word, you can observe these kinds of *sight data*:

- context — location and who is present
- time — when during the day and promptness or delay in response
- space — physical position of people (closeness or distance), clutter or orderly arrangement
- body language — posture, eye contact, facial expressions, hand and arm gestures, general body movements
- energy level — alertness, involvement, fatigue
- objects — dishes, furniture, paper, equipment
- clothing — formal or informal, neat or unkempt
- media — television, newspaper

Sound data include:

- background noise — people talking, radio, television, appliances running
- rate and pace of speech — slow, medium, or fast; steady or halting
- pitch and tone — low, medium, or high; flat, fluctuating, strained, strong, or confident
- volume of voice — soft, medium, loud
- diction and clarity — precise, mumbling

Touch (hard, soft; hot, cold; rigid, flexible; smooth, scratchy), *smell,* and *taste* are important sources of nonverbal data, too.

Intuitive Sensations

Another important kind of data is that of intuitive sensations — "data" that do not come from your immediate, external, physical world but rather from your internal world of memories, associations, insights, knowings, dreams, hunches, and so forth. When one of these intuitive sensations occurs, it may be difficult to document your perceptions with physical data. This is true in part because intuitive sensations often draw on bits or fragments of both internal and external data. However, when pressed to describe the source of their information, most people can describe specific internal or external sensations.

THOUGHTS — The Meaning You Make

Thoughts are the meanings you make to help you understand yourself, other people, and situations. You form thoughts from the *beliefs* you bring to a situation, the *interpretations* you make of immediate and recollected sensory data, and the *expectations* and anticipation you have of the future. Other words that signal thinking processes include:

attitudes	evaluations	predictions	needs
assumptions	judgments	objections	values
conclusions	impressions	principles	reasons
opinions	ideas	rules	benefits

This zone of the Awareness Wheel refers to the logical, analytical, and rational process of weighing data to arrive at a conclusion. However, sometimes thoughts can be quite illogical.

When issues arise, your beliefs, interpretations, and expectations play a part in them. Recognizing these influences helps you to understand the issues better.

Beliefs

The beliefs you bring from past experience either limit or expand what can grow out of a circumstance. Beliefs are powerful. They influence your perceptions — what you actually see and hear — as well as other parts of your Awareness Wheel.

For example, your self-esteem is a distillation of your beliefs and judgments about yourself in different circumstances across time. If you judge yourself to be innovative, competent, and responsible, you will carry confidence into different situations. Likewise, if you have doubts about your abilities, you will broadcast this self-evaluation as well. In this way, beliefs often become self-fulfilling prophesies.

Interpretations

Whereas beliefs represent what you bring to a situation, interpretations are the meanings you make out of sensory data you perceive at the moment. We use this term to include the analysis of facts.

Interpretations represent the way you put your world together — the way you make sense out of data. What is real for you counts. Others may see and hear the same data and come to very different conclusions. For example, you and your partner walk into your house and see dirty dishes scattered around. You think your twelve-year-old has been irresponsible for not cleaning up after himself. Your partner, however, thinks your son has been quite responsible and has shown initiative to make a meal on his own.

Expectations

Expectations are what you think will happen. You expect — think — that you will meet your partner at two o'clock. Following a conversation about table manners, you expect a more relaxing dinner with the kids. An expectation is an anticipated experience — waiting to happen.

In the process of forming thoughts, it is easy to filter (delete) or imagine (add) data because other zones of your Awareness Wheel influence your thoughts.

FEELINGS — Your Emotional Responses

Feelings are your spontaneous physiological responses to the match between your sensory data and your thoughts or wants in a situation. Your senses are constantly scanning the environment for signs of fulfilled or unfulfilled expectations and desires. The match or mismatch between your external input and your internal evaluation triggers positive or negative emotions. The greater your expectations and desires, the stronger the resulting feelings.

For instance, if you are expecting to receive a particular job offer and it goes to someone else, you might feel hurt, angry, and jealous. On the other hand, you might feel a little relieved, if part of you believed the job might be over your head or too demanding.

Emotional responses register in your body. Your body gives clues to your feelings. For example, anger shows in tight muscles and flushed skin, and it sounds loud and strident in speech. When you are contented, your breathing is deep and slow; muscles in your face, neck, and shoulders are relaxed.

To help you identify some common emotions, here is a partial list of feeling words:

happy	proud	lonely	disappointed
sad	trusting	annoyed	eager
satisfied	confident	comfortable	disinterested
angry	frustrated	uneasy	fascinated
peaceful	excited	sexy	bored
fearful	hesitant	irritated	surprised
hurt	anxious	jealous	glad

The more your positive expectations and desires are fulfilled, the more the feelings you experience are likely to be pleasant ones. However, the more you do not know what to expect, the more uncertain and anxious you feel. (Uncertainty is a major cause of stress disorders.) And, repeated expectations or desires without fulfillment lead to anger and depression.

Feelings Are Information

Some people think that feelings are irrational and hard to understand. Actually, they are really quite predictable, "rational" information. Your feelings, whatever they are, reflect what is going on in the other parts of your Awareness Wheel. Unless they are distorted by a chemical deficiency or imbalance in your body or by drug abuse, feelings do not just suddenly appear out of a vacuum.

Feelings are information about you at any moment — important in their own right. They do not have to be justified, denied, or avoided. They are a part of "what is." When you overlook or do not attend to your feelings, you miss important self-information.

When you consider your feelings, it is common to think of having just one feeling. More often however, several feelings operate at the same time, such as frustration, disappointment, and irritation. And feelings are not always all negative or positive. Frequently they are mixed. Each specific feeling is associated with a particular thought or fragment of a cluster of expectations.

Feelings About Feelings

Most of us have feelings about feelings. For example, we feel embarrassed about fear of closeness; guilt about anger or pride; shame about envy and jealousy. In effect, these are beliefs that we have learned about our feelings — that we should feel embarrassed, guilty, and so forth. Recognize that your feelings about feelings can interfere with your awareness of how you actually feel at any point in time.

Using Your Feelings

You do not have to be out of control or weak to have feelings. Quite the contrary, recognizing your feelings is a resource for managing yourself.

When you acknowledge your feelings, they typically lose their power over you. Connecting with your own feelings, especially in tough situations, is central to your wellness and effective communication.

WANTS — Your Desires

Wants are your desires and wishes for yourself, for others, and for your relationship together. Wants can be small or large, short-term or long-term. They generally imply a moving toward or moving away from something or someone.

Some common words associated with wants include:

goals	hopes	interests	wishes
objectives	drives	targets	dreams
motives	intentions	desires	likes

Think of your wants as mini-plans — your priorities. They often start as a dream or fantasy and are translated into specific goals and objectives. They can be shuffled about and reordered as you consider alternatives. They are tentative until translated into action.

Wants Are Motivators

Everybody wants something! Wants motivate and energize you and others from moment to moment. When you connect with your wants, you focus your energy and release a strong force. Not knowing what you want can keep you stuck.

Three basic types of wants, with examples, include:

1. To *be:* honest, respected, liked, appreciated, successful, healthy, helpful.

2. To *do* — *general*: compete, win, collaborate, get even, ignore, clarify, destroy, demand, listen, persuade, understand, undermine, support.

   To *do* — *specific*: finish a project, read the newspaper, talk to your spouse, cook supper, increase income, change job.

3. To *have*: a good education, a stimulating job, satisfying relationships, a happy family, good friends, a nice car, money in savings.

As with feelings, wants are often held in combination. They vary in intensity and can be in conflict with one another. For example, part of me wants to be with you, and part of me wants to be by myself right now. Fragmented and conflicting wants can work against you, scattering energy.

Wants For Self, Partner, Us

Wants can benefit me, my partner, and us.

Wants For Me — My Self

Most of the time when we think of wants, we think of ourselves: what I want for myself.

Wants For Other(s) — My Partner

When it comes to thinking about others, often we think about what we want from others (for self) — not for others. However, the difference between *from* and *for* is big, and it has implications for how you relate to your partner and other significant people in your life.

When you think about what you want *from* others, you are still really thinking about what you want for yourself. Your attention is focused on what they can do to help you achieve your own desires. (The things or actions you want from other people can easily become something you demand of them.)

When you think about what you want positively *for* others, with no strings attached, you are truly in their court. Thinking about their interests

— what they have said they want — instead of your own interests captures the notion of wants for others. Thinking about what you truly want for your partner reflects your caring for him or her.

For example, suppose you are a person who is not particularly punctual, but being on time is important to your partner. Making a special effort to arrive at events or appointments on schedule is something you can do for your partner. You may not experience any immediate personal benefits from your action; nevertheless, out of respect or love for your partner, you transcend your own interests and do it for him or her.

Wants For Us — Our Relationship

To think about wants for your relationship, consider, "What's in this for us — as a pair or family?" Here you think of yourself and others as members of a larger unit, focusing on wants for the bigger entity. Usually wants at this level are to increase mutual confidence, trust, and esprit de corps, to enhance your love and affection for each other, or to be successful together.

Your intentions for yourself, your partner, and your relationship have dramatic impact on your communication. This is because what you want, consciously or unconsciously, comes out directly or indirectly in your actions, the next part of the Awareness Wheel.

ACTIONS — Your Behavior

The action zone of the Awareness Wheel includes:

Past Action: what you have said or done or were doing earlier (yesterday, last week, or last year).

Present Action: what you are currently saying or doing.

Future Action: what specifically you will do later (next hour, tomorrow, or next week); the commitments you make.

Actions are your behavioral output; they are the results of how you process sensory data, your thoughts, your feelings, and your wants. They are what you choose to do.

Think of actions as:

behaviors	plans	accomplishments
statements	promises	consequences
activities	proposals	achievements

Most of us are conscious of these broader categories of actions, but we are often less aware of the little things we do that punctuate our conversation: the pauses, foot-tappings, frowning, finger-pointing, or laughing. All of this output becomes sensory data for the perceptions others have of us.

Future Actions

This is the point at which you make choices and commitments — to do or not to do, to say or not to say. Choosing and exercising options requires the conscious act of your will.

Future actions are what you will do. Future actions carry a definite commitment to act.

USING YOUR AWARENESS WHEEL

When sensory data (external cues) or your thoughts, feelings, or wants (internal cues) tell you something unexpected is going on or will probably occur, an issue is at hand.

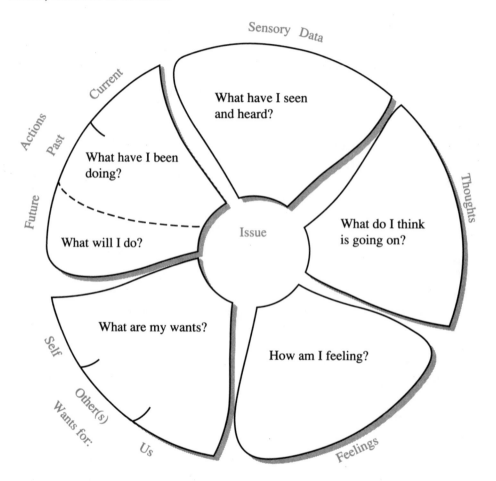

Issues usually arise as:

- Surprising observations
- Unclear, confusing, or disturbing thoughts
- Uncomfortable feelings
- Unfulfilled or conflicting wants
- Inappropriate actions or inaction

When issues arise, one of the ways of using the Awareness Wheel is in self-talk about the particular issue. The other is by applying specific talking skills to communicate your awareness.

SELF-TALK

Self-Talk is the private reflection and internal monologue you have about the past, current, and future aspects of an issue. You ask yourself, "What's gone on and is going on right now? What is my experience?" Use your Awareness Wheel to access and expand your awareness.

Illustration

Here is the way one person used the Awareness Wheel in self-talk to expand his awareness about an issue. In this instance, an issue had been festering inside of Tom for quite some time. He was the manager of a district office of a large national advertising agency, and his issue revolved around whether to quit his job and start his own company or stay with his firm.

Past and Current Actions:

Tom had worked in the field for fifteen years, five with one organization and ten with his current company. He had been a manager for twelve of those years. He recently consulted an attorney regarding non-compete aspects in the contract he had signed with his firm.

Sensory Data:

Tom saw the profit and loss statements, and he watched about 60 percent of the revenue go to the home office. He looked around at other independent ventures in the field, including one by his predecessor at his firm, and he saw that a number of these people still remained in business. Others had gone under, however.

Tom also looked at his own income and benefits. He made a six-figure income, drove a comfortable car paid for by the agency, and heard from his superiors that his place in the organization would stay secure even if a business downturn might occur.

Thoughts

Tom thought that being part of a large organization had its negatives and positives. While he lacked freedom to make major policy decisions, he recognized that his job was secure. He realized that acquiring finances for a company he might start would require personal risks. He figured that a lot of waste occurred in his present company, but the business remained highly profitable. He also considered how he would use his time to best advantage during a waiting period of non-competition.

Feelings

Tom felt constricted and frustrated working for the large organization. He also felt unappreciated and irritated when his suggestions went unheeded. He was tired and sometimes depressed. Tom felt guilty, too, for thinking about leaving the company and was concerned for his staff.

Wants

Tom wanted to take his time but eventually make a move to start his own advertising company. He also wanted to stay secure financially and to maintain the friendships among the staff at his present company. He wanted to prepare them for the eventual competition he would bring.

Future Action

Tom decided to make a business plan. He would sit with an accountant and then a banker to determine the amount of money he would need to go on his own. He also decided to talk with his wife about his feelings and the seeming mix of the wants he held.

The Awareness Wheel can improve your self-talk by helping you recognize and understand the five zones of self-information. This understanding allows you to increase your choices regarding the issue.

TALKING SKILLS

If you decide to share your self-information based on the Awareness Wheel, here are six basic talking skills that will help you to do so more clearly and directly. These skills will help you let your partner know what is going on inside you at a given point in time. They are:

1. Speak for Self

2. Describe Sensory Data

3. Express Thoughts

4. Share Feelings

5. Disclose Wants

6. State Actions

1. SPEAK FOR SELF

To speak for self, the first skill, is basic to all the other talking skills. When you speak for yourself, you combine a personal pronoun — "I," "me," "my," or "mine" — with any part(s) of your Awareness Wheel to form a message.

"I want more time to think about it."

"Your response really pleases me."

"Here's my idea."

"I'll call you Thursday."

To speak for self indicates that you take responsibility for what you say and that you own your statements. As a result, your messages are clearer and easier for others to hear. In turn, people are more apt to accept what you say as your experience and less apt to discount your thoughts, feelings, and wants.

Speaking for self does not mean you focus only on your own activities, interests, and concerns. You may express your awareness about any kind of content: "I'm puzzled by the weather" (focus-topic); "My tooth cracked today" (focus-yourself); "Your story is fascinating to me. Tell me more" (focus-other); "I want our relationship to be satisfying for both of us" (focus-relationship).

Over-Responsible "You Statements"

An alternative to speaking for self is speaking for others. When you speak for other people, you use words like "you," "we," or "everyone." You stimulate defensiveness in others and resistance to what you say simply by the way you say it. Others hear your words as trying to "box them in" by controlling what they think, feel, or want.

"That's not what you really think."

"You're not listening."

"Now you're angry."

"We don't believe that."

"Everyone knows better."

When you speak for others, you work against your own objectives because few people like someone else running their lives, no matter how small the attempt. Most people find it invasive, pushy, and manipulative, even if what is said is true or is something they might normally accept.

Speaking for others is heard as rigid pronouncements rather than as personal experience with room for difference. Your partner probably has to recoil, defend, and protect himself or herself against your invasion.

On the other hand, when you speak for yourself, you count yourself and respect others, giving them room to be themselves.

Under-Responsible "No-One" Statements

Another alternative to speaking for self is speaking for no one. These messages lack clarity and directness. They can leave you guessing about who the talker really is and what the meaning is.

"No-one" statements have no juice. The impact they make is cold and distant. By substituting "it," "some people," or "one" for "I," they speak for no one.

"It might be good for us to be more open with each other."

"One could get upset about this."

These messages are voiced in an indirect, cautious, and uncommitted way. The person talking does not appear to value the messages. Others soon devalue the opinions, intentions, and feelings, too.

In short, speaking for self helps you send clearer messages which are easier for others to hear.

2. DESCRIBE SENSORY DATA

To describe sensory data, you tell what you see, hear, touch, taste, and smell — your input from the external world. This is usually information about something or somebody. When you describe sensory data, you provide concrete examples of what you have observed at a *particular time* or *place*. The more specific the sensory data, the more useful it is.

In interpersonal situations, describing sensory data means telling about another person's actions — specific verbal and nonverbal behaviors — not your own actions.

"I hear a lilt in your voice right now."

"I noticed everyone became very quiet this morning after you proposed that we stop exchanging gifts during the holidays."

Sensory data also include facts, figures, and information from print and other sources.

"The market was up eleven points today."

In addition, sensory data can be about your own bodily sensations, such as temperature or pain.

Documenting — Linking Observations to Interpretations

Documenting simply means providing specific sensory data with your thoughts. Describing your specific database orients others and gives them a chance to tell you how they are interpreting the same data. Compare these two statements:

"You're tired." (This speaking-for-other interpretation may spark a sharp retort such as, "Well, I'm not!")

"I see dark circles under your eyes this morning. You look tired to me. I notice you've been putting in twelve- and fourteen-hour days for the last six weeks." (Speaking for self and giving sensory data make this message much clearer and easier to hear.)

Sensory data can be used in an argument to try to prove a point, or they can be used in a discussion to help create understanding. How you use sensory data all depends on your attitude and your intentions.

3. EXPRESS THOUGHTS

To express your thoughts is simply the act of saying what it is you are thinking — believing, interpreting, or expecting.

"I believe it's very important."

"It seems possible to me."

"I think you will enjoy it."

"I expect to be on time."

Expressing your thoughts clearly is important because thinking is an ongoing process. You are constantly creating, perpetuating, modifying, or discarding ideas. Expressing your thoughts lets others know where you are in the process, cutting down on inaccurate assumptions others make about you.

4. SHARE FEELINGS

To share feelings means stating your emotions directly. These kinds of statements add seasoning to your communication.

Most of the time you can accurately report your feelings without using the phrase, "I feel":

"I'm really happy about the way we worked together redecorating this place."

"My disappointment will die down, but it's strong right now."

"I sure am relieved to hear that from you!"

"I'm proud of you and really thrilled by your success."

Do not confuse "what you think" with "how you feel." People often use the word "feel" for "think," believing that they have expressed their feelings. But this is not so. For example, "I feel that we made a good decision" does not report a feeling, only a thought. "I feel confident because I think we made a good decision" is a feeling statement with a thought statement. Usually, the phrase, "I feel that . . ." signals a thought, rather than a feeling.

On occasion, a metaphor can be a very effective way to let others know your emotions: "I have butterflies"; "I feel like I was just 'shot out of the saddle' "; "I feel like an eagle, floating on air."

Feelings are commonly expressed through nonverbal behavior: buying a gift; staying away; kissing; laughing; crying; slamming doors; or storming around. Nonverbal expressions of feelings can have high impact, but they can also be very unclear. Explicitly stating the feelings associated with your behavior makes your action much clearer.

5. DISCLOSE WANTS

Disclosing wants and desires lets others know in a direct way what you desire *to be, to do,* or *to have.* When you make intention statements, use words such as, "I want . . .," "I don't want . . .," "I'd like . . .," "I intend . . ." Here are some examples:

"I want to be fair (to be)."

"I hope to climb as many peaks over 14,000 feet this summer as I can (to do)."

"I'd like to have a faster computer with more memory (to have)."

Saying What You Want for Self, Your Partner, and Us

Disclosing wants also involves clearly identifying what you want *for* whom. For example:

Wants for me — myself

"I want to relax a while."

"I'd like you to listen to my idea."

"I want to eat out tonight."

Wants for other(s) — my partner

"I would like for you to have your own car."

"I want you to feel appreciated."

"I'd like for you to change jobs if you wish."

Wants for us — our relationship

"I would like for us to really be able to count on each other."

"I want us to have a good time together."

"I wish we could make more money."

Verbally expressing your wants for other(s) — your partner's interests and your relationship — is a bonding force that transcends self interests.

Sometimes people use the word *need* to express a *want:* "I need to have you . . ."; however, *need* is a tricky word. Often it has a manipulative quality that tends to overstate the situation, which can create resistance to your want. If you really do think you need something, give your reasons and explain what might happen if your need is not met. Otherwise, use "I need" sparingly as a want statement.

By disclosing wants, you invite your partner's help in making them a reality. Being direct about what you want or would like does not guarantee that you will get it. But it does make your wants negotiable and minimizes the possibility of unpleasant surprises for your partner when your hidden agenda (unstated wants) emerge from the shadows.

6. STATE ACTIONS

Action statements describe your behavior — what you *have* done, *are* doing, or *will* do. They refer to your own past, current, or future behaviors.

"I called you yesterday afternoon, but didn't get an answer."

"I was thinking about something at the office and didn't hear what you said."

"I believe you."

"I will make the decision by three p.m."

Are these statements really necessary? Is your behavior not obvious to everyone? No, it is not always apparent. Consider this action statement, "I was thinking about something at the office and didn't hear what you said." The only thing obvious to my partner was that I was sitting motionless, staring off into space. My partner may or may not be able to guess that the reason I was not listening was my preoccupation with thoughts about the office. My action statement makes guessing unnecessary.

Furthermore, action statements let others know that you are aware of your behavior. For example, when I say to my son, "I interrupted you," my statement lets him know that I care about the impact of my action on him. It is a way of saying, "You are important to me."

Stating your actions also lets others know the meaning you assign to your own behavior: "I'm yawning because I didn't get to bed until after two o'clock. I'm not bored with our conversation."

Stating Actions Builds Trust and Confidence

Stating what you will do in the future lets others know that you are accountable. Notice the difference between saying, "I might," "I could," or "I want to," and, clearly committing yourself to action, saying "I will." *Commitment* distinguishes skill number 6 (stating actions) from skill number 5 (disclosing wants).

SENDING CLEARER MESSAGES

The key to speaking effectively about an issue is using all the talking skills, in any order or combination, to disclose your experience completely and clearly. A statement does not need to be lengthy. However, as you talk, combine two or more parts of the Wheel.

"I'm concerned (feeling) about our spending (action). I noticed the balance in our savings account is at its lowest level in two years (sensory data). If we don't do something to reduce our expenses (action), I think we could be in big trouble needlessly (thought)."

Notice how each part of the message adds new information.

"I wasn't sure (feeling) about my wanting to go (want). So I haven't said anything about it (action) since the first time you mentioned it last week (sensory data). More importantly (thought), I've been afraid (feeling) to turn you down (action), because I think I might offend you (thought). And I don't want to do that (want)."

For clearer statements, send concise, multi-part messages that cover three or more zones of your Wheel.

Caring About Yourself

The first step in caring about yourself is attending to your own experience — valuing and trusting what your body, mind, and spirit are telling you. Knowing yourself is not the same as being selfish and self-centered. Self-awareness is using the most personal resources you have for the development of understanding and wisdom in life and relationships.

Connecting with all parts of your experience — sensory data, thoughts, feelings, wants, and actions — is powerful without trying to be powerful. Acting congruently on your self-awareness generates personal energy, strength, and health.

LIST OF CURRENT ISSUES

Date _____

Instructions: Take five minutes, relax, and think about what is going on in your life at the present time. Think of your concerns at home, at work, and elsewhere. As you reflect, write down a word or phrase to represent each issue that comes into your mind. This is an opportunity to step back and see what's important to you at this point in time. (You may wish to review the topical, personal, and relational list of issues in the Introduction, page 7, to help you identify your issues.)

Issues

SELF-TALK — ORGANIZING YOUR AWARENESS

Instructions: Choose a topical or personal issue (not a relational issue with your partner) from your list of issues (on the previous page) that you would be willing to talk about in the group. Tell your partner your choice. Write the issue in the hub of the Awareness Wheel below. Next, answer the questions related to each zone of the Wheel with key words or phrases that represent your experience/awareness of the issue.

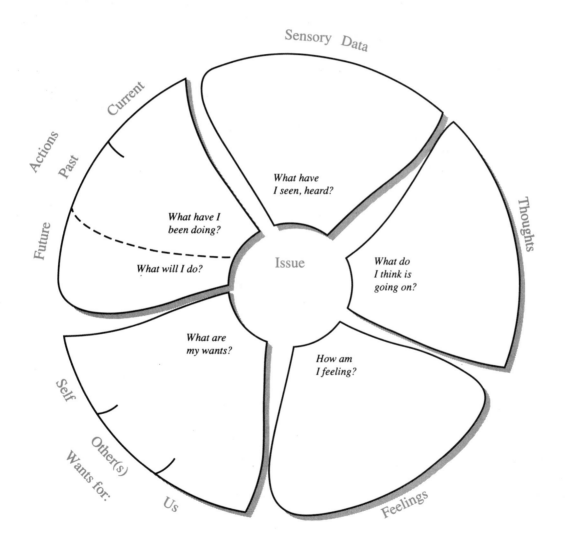

USING THE AWARENESS WHEEL SKILLS MAT

Background Information

Skills mats (available directly from your instructor or ICP, Inc.) are tools to help you learn communication skills faster and better. The Awareness Wheel mat provides a practical structure for organizing, prompting, and expressing your awareness. By physically stepping from zone to zone on the Awareness Wheel, you can access deeper, clearer, and more complete information about yourself.

Use the Awareness Wheel Skills Mat:

For Self-Talk

- Reviewing a past situation
- Reflecting on a current issue
- Anticipating a future event

For Sending Clearer Messages

- Rehearsing what you want to say
- Expressing your awareness clearly, directly, and accurately

For Coaching/Teaching Skills

- Focusing observation
- Prompting awareness
- Giving feedback

OBSERVING/COACHING A PERSON ON THE AWARENESS WHEEL SKILLS MAT

To Observe:

- Focus on skills (zones of the Awareness Wheel).

- Look for:

   Accuracy — the clear use of skills (statement matching zone).

- Notice:

   Pattern — sequence of movement among zones.

   Completeness — coverage of all zones of the Awareness Wheel.

   Nonverbals — significant tones and movements.

- Use the observation/coaching worksheet (see next page) to jot down notes (key words, phrases, gestures) for feedback later.

To Coach:

- Ask the person on the mat if he or she would like some coaching. If so:

- Encourage the talker to step onto the zone he or she is expressing, if he or she is not on the corresponding zone.

- Direct the person occasionally to a specific zone and encourage him or her to expand that awareness.

- Ask the talker, if appropriate, if you may "be him or her." Then briefly step onto a zone or two suggesting the talker's possible experience, if he or she is unclear about his or her awareness. Be careful not to superimpose solutions, advice, or interpretations, however.

- Give brief feedback by using the talking skills yourself. Do not pressure or force awareness.

OBSERVING/COACHING A PERSON ON THE AWARENESS WHEEL SKILLS MAT

Instructions: Listen for clear, accurate skill statements that correspond with the zones on the mat that the talker steps into as he or she talks about an issue. Use the Wheels below to jot down the talker's words or phrases (for feedback later) that indicate clear use of a talking skill in the zone(s) you are observing.

Person: _____

Other observations:

Person: _____

Other observations:

TALKING SKILLS ACTION PLAN

Instructions: Here is a list of the talking skills taught in Chapter 1. Complete the following steps:

Step 1. Without consulting your partner, mark each item with an "X" to represent your current use of each talking skill.

When you are with your partner, how often do you:	Seldom				Often	
1. Speak for Self?	1	2	3	4	5	6
2. Describe Sensory Data?	1	2	3	4	5	6
3. Express Thoughts?	1	2	3	4	5	6
4. Share Feelings?	1	2	3	4	5	6
5. Disclose Wants for:						
Self?	1	2	3	4	5	6
Partner?	1	2	3	4	5	6
Us?	1	2	3	4	5	6
6. State Actions?	1	2	3	4	5	6

Step 2. Choose and list one or two skills to practice between now and the next session.

Skill: _____

Skill: _____

Step 3. Compare your choices with your partner, and talk about where and when each of you will practice using the skills.

Between Sessions

Step 4. When you notice your partner using the talking skill(s) he or she has chosen to practice between sessions, give your partner some positive feedback for using the skill(s). Encourage your partner by telling how the skill makes his or her messages clearer and increases your understanding (even if it is a difficult message to receive).

SELF-TALK USING THE AWARENESS WHEEL SKILLS MAT

Set some time to be alone in a quiet place and use the Awareness Wheel skills mat to do self-talk.

See your list of issues on page 38 and use the mat to:

- Review a past situation

- Reflect on a current issue

- Anticipate a future event

Directions

1. Be sure the mat does not slip on the floor when you step on it. Set the mat so that you can read the words (facing you) as you look down.

2. Stand on the "issue" at center, and identify the issue, if possible.

3. Move to whatever zone (for example, thoughts, feelings, wants, and so on) corresponds with what you are experiencing. Let yourself fully experience that zone.

4. Move criss-cross or clockwise, (sometimes rather quickly) as awareness comes to you. Be sure your reflections accurately correspond with the zone on which you are standing. (For example, step on "thoughts" when you think thoughts and on "feelings" when you feel emotions.) If you are unclear about the nature of a zone, review the description in Chapter 1.

5. Use any zone to prompt or expand your awareness of the issue.

6. Continue to move from zone to zone until your awareness is complete. (Sometimes you may find that it is not necessary to move to future action, however. The self-talk process may simply bring understanding of an issue, rather than what to do about it at the moment. Sometimes understanding is the outcome.)

7. Step off of the mat, and stop processing your awareness, whenever you wish.

TALKING SKILLS — USING AWARENESS WHEEL SKILLS MAT WITH YOUR PARTNER

Arrange for some private time together with your partner to share one of your topical or personal issues. (See your list of issues on page 38.) Use this time as a talking-skill practice session and not as a consultation or an issue-resolving exchange.

Use the Awareness Wheel skills mat to:

- Express your awareness clearly, directly, and accurately.

Directions

1. Be sure the mat does not slip on the floor when you step on it. Set the mat so that you can read the words (facing you) as you look down.

2. Ask your partner just to observe and coach you on your use of talking skills, and not to react to or advise you about the issue.

3. Move to the center of the mat and identify your issue. Give general background information about the issue or situation, if necessary.

4. Step to whatever zone (for example, thoughts, feelings, wants, and so on) corresponds with what you are experiencing, and share your awareness by speaking for yourself.

5. Continue to talk about the issue by stepping from zone to zone on the Wheel. Move criss-cross or clockwise, as awareness comes to you. Be sure your statements accurately correspond with the zone on which you are standing. If you are unclear about the nature of a zone, review the description in Chapter 1.

6. Move continually from zone to zone until you have completely expressed yourself. Moving to future action is not always necessary, however. You may simply disclose your understanding of the issue, rather than what you will do about it at the moment.

7. Step off the mat, and stop processing your awareness, whenever you wish.

8. Thank your partner for observing and coaching.

SENDING A CLEAR AND COMPLETE MESSAGE

Instructions: Use the Awareness Wheel below to organize your awareness about an important message you want to communicate to someone.

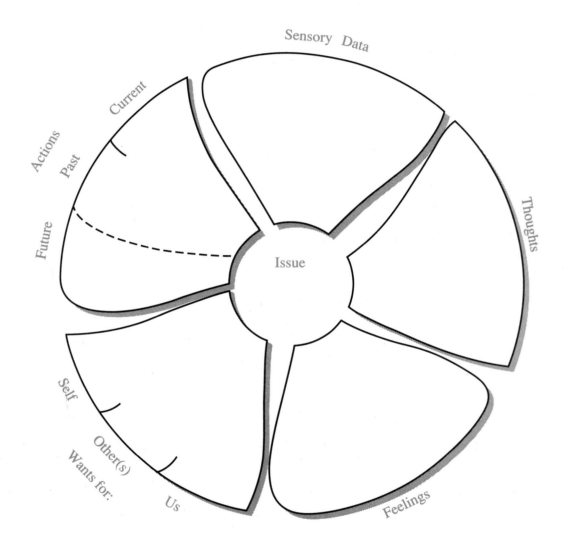

Rehearse your message by speaking for self and using the other talking skills.

TALKING SKILLS IDENTIFICATION

Each of the fifteen statements below combines the skill "speaking for self" with one of the five zones of the Awareness Wheel, resulting in one of the other talking skills. Identify the talking skill in each statement by placing the letter for the skill on the line provided.

a) Describe Sensory Data   d) Disclose Wants
b) Express Thoughts   e) State Actions
c) Share Feelings

Answer

1. I'd like to set aside time to talk about our vacation next week.   _____

2. I get angry and frustrated when you say one thing and do another.   _____

3. I don't believe she cares.   _____

4. Wow, was I excited to hear from you!   _____

5. I expect a good report.   _____

6. I didn't go last week.   _____

7. I notice you're leaning back in your chair, not smiling.   _____

8. I think you misunderstood her.   _____

9. I'll call Jim tomorrow morning.   _____

10. I'm confident about it.   _____

11. I wish I would hear from her.   _____

12. I smell your perfume.   _____

13. I intend to look into that soon.   _____

14. I'm reading a magazine now.   _____

15. I heard you say at dinner that you were interested in going with us.   _____

The answers are:

1.d, 2.c, 3.b, 4.c, 5.b, 6.e, 7.a, 8.b, 9.e, 10.c, 11.d, 12.a, 13.d, 14.e, 15.a

ACTIONS FOR CARING ABOUT YOURSELF

How have you been caring and not caring about yourself physically, emotionally, relationally, and spiritually over the past week?

Directions: Use the space below to make notes about what (actions) you have been doing in each of these areas.

	Caring	Not Caring
Physically		
Emotionally		
Relationally		
Spiritually		

REVIEW YOUR TALKING SKILLS ACTION PLAN AND LEARNING GOALS

How are you doing with your Session 1 Action Plan (see page 43) and your overall Learning Goals (see page 12)? How do these fit with caring about yourself? Be sure you are putting your plans and goals to work for you.

CARING
ABOUT
YOUR
PARTNER

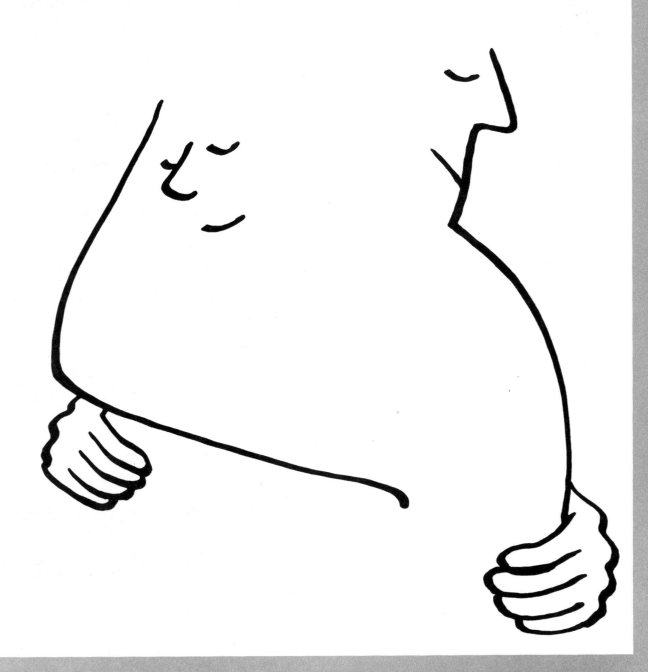

2

Caring About Your Partner

LISTENING TO UNDERSTAND

In the first chapter, we showed you how to use the Awareness Wheel map to understand yourself better, and to apply six specific talking skills to disclose your self-awareness. You can also use the map to understand your partner better. In this chapter, we will add listening skills to help you gain emotional as well as intellectual understanding of your partner.

When you use the listening skills, you demonstrate an I-care-about-you attitude. And, when you and your partner use both the talking and the listening skills, drawing on the Awareness Wheel, you will find that your exchanges become clearer with fewer misunderstandings.

Most of us have habits which keep us from paying full attention to the talker when there is a stressful or complicated issue. Often we pay only partial attention because we are rehearsing our next speech instead. At other times, as we listen, we mainly evaluate what the other person is saying. We form judgments about whether it is right or wrong, good or bad, or whether we agree or disagree. We compare our own viewpoint with the other person's. Our behavior is more reactive than attentive, and we find it easy to interrupt — whether by statements or questions. When we listen in these ways, we keep ourselves front and center, and focus our attention more on our own experience than on the other person's.

The key to listening is following!

Good listening puts your own concerns on hold temporarily and encourages your partner be the leader — to tell his or her full story spontaneously, without your interference. *Your goal is understanding — without necessarily agreeing or disagreeing, blaming or defending, or jumping into action (posing a solution).*

LISTENING SKILLS

Here are five skills that will help you improve your listening ability:

1. Attend

2. Acknowledge

3. Invite

4. Summarize

5. Ask

The following section describes each listening skill in more detail.

1. ATTEND: Look, Listen, Track

When you attend to your partner, you give him or her your full attention by listening with your body and your mind. Stop other activity that could be distracting. If your partner is sitting, sit. If he or she is standing, stand. Turn your body toward your partner and give him or her eye contact (when possible). On occasion you may want to touch your partner supportively as well.

In general, let your partner set the pace. In attending, you are putting your concerns aside for the moment, and giving your partner the floor. This values him or her by signaling your availability, receptivity, and interest.

As you listen, try to take in as much sensory data as you can. Carefully attending to your partner's words and actions (verbal and nonverbal messages) becomes the basis for your interpretations and for understanding him or her at the moment. Do this by *looking, listening, and tracking* while your partner talks.

Look, Listen, and Track

Look at the nonverbals. Watch your partner's facial and body movements, as well as posture shifts and breathing. If you let your eyes soften their focus, you will be able to see more of the nonverbal communication — the small facial, hand, and muscle movements, as well as the breathing rate. Observe the closeness or distance and the space between you. Also notice the context — where you are.

Listen to the sounds. Listen for the speech tones and inflections, as well as the rate and pitch of the voice. Hear the softness, loudness, and level of tension as your partner talks. As you listen to the words, notice any images, figures of speech, or metaphors he or she may use.

Track the zones of the Awareness Wheel that your partner discloses. Notice, for instance, if your partner tells you something he or she has seen or heard (sensory data), a new idea (thought), something exciting (feeling), a special desire (want), or perhaps something he or she is doing (action). All these parts add to your understanding of your partner. Also, recognize any significant shifts from one zone of the Awareness Wheel to the next.

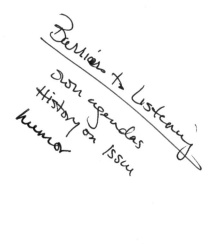

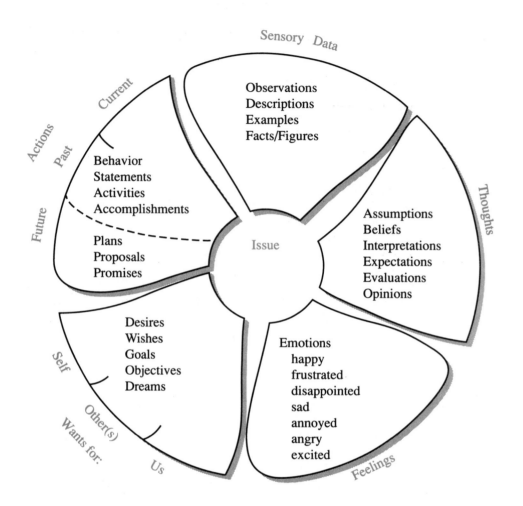

As you track the messages, take note whether any zone of the Awareness Wheel is missing — not spoken. For instance, your partner may give you facts and ideas, or even propose a future action, but not tell feelings or wants. Attend to what is left unsaid, too.

In your looking, listening, and tracking, notice the matches and mismatches between the verbal and the nonverbal messages. Incongruencies (mismatches) appear when the words do not match the accompanying body movements or tone of voice. For example, your partner may say he or she is interested in doing something, but the expression on the face and a sigh do not seem to agree with the words.

To be an effective listener, attend to the talker, taking in both words and actions, rather than rehearsing your next statement. As you see, hear, and follow, you will be filling out your own moment-by-moment sensory data about your partner. These data become the basis for responding in a way that helps you connect better.

2. ACKNOWLEDGE Other's Experience

Acknowledging someone else's messages is a response that lets the person know verbally and nonverbally that you are with him or her, and that he or she is leading and you are following. When you show interest in and respect for what your partner is saying, you validate your partner's experience, even though you may not fully agree with it.

An acknowledgement can range from a simple nod of your head or an "uh-huh" to making a brief interpretative statement that reflects what you think your partner is experiencing but has not stated explicitly. Examples of acknowledging include:

"That sounds important."

"I can see you're really concerned."

"The idea must really be exciting."

"I guess you don't really want to go."

When your acknowledgement taps your partner's experience accurately, the impact can be powerful. His or her response to your acknowledgement shows if you have touched the right chord. If so, your partner receives your acceptance, understanding, and affirmation — empathy.

Tune into your partner's energy. In listening, the key information at any moment is where the other person's energy is, not where yours is. In your acknowledging, move to the point of his or her energy. To do that, join your partner in the zone of the Awareness Wheel he or she is emphasizing. For example, if your partner is talking about an idea, acknowledge the idea. If he or she is talking about an action or describing sensory data, acknowledge those.

Acknowledge what's not said, especially the zones in the lower parts of the Wheel. Most conversations focus on data, thoughts, and actions — the upper parts of the Awareness Wheel. The powerful lower portions of the Wheel — feelings and wants — often go unexpressed and unacknowledged. Try not to let this happen.

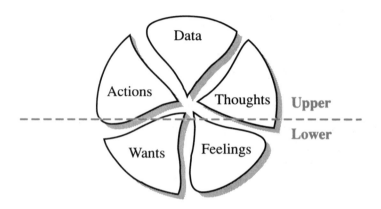

Many people mistakenly believe the upper part of the Wheel is rational and understandable while the lower part is irrational and unmanageable. The facts are that thoughts can be quite irrational, and that feelings are logical and understandable. Feelings are logical in the sense that they reflect what is going on in the rest of the Wheel. It is true, however, that wants can be quite irrational.

No amount of rational talk above the line will satisfy a festering feeling or want below the line. Acknowledging the unexpressed feelings and wants releases the tension and brings that crucial information into the conversation.

Occasionally you will find your partner talking about an issue but not expressing his or her full Awareness Wheel. Your partner may not be conscious of all the parts or may be hesitant to disclose parts. Fill in what is not said based on the sensory data you are receiving.

For example, based on the data you pick up as you look, listen, and track, you might say, "Sounds like you're really upset," after your partner has described something that has happened. You are making an interpretation. You will see from your partner's response if your acknowledgement is accurate or not.

Be aware of your intentions. If the intention behind your acknowledgement is to change your partner's experience or subtly persuade him or her to agree with your perspective, you will be speaking for your partner (rather than for yourself) and trying to put words into his or her mouth. This manipulation won't work. You will fail to connect since there is no real understanding or respect evident on your part. Your partner will verbally or nonverbally resist your reflections. Your interpretation will be distracting rather than helpful.

Acknowledging builds bridges by conveying your acceptance of your partner's right to say what he or she is experiencing at that moment. In effect, you are "going with" — rather than "against" by blocking, sidetracking, or reacting to — what is disclosed. Often just acknowledging what the other person is experiencing is all that is necessary to connect and create understanding.

3. INVITE More Information

For this listening skill, you simply say or do something that encourages your partner to continue spontaneously talking about whatever it is he or she wants to tell you. Inviting goes a step beyond acknowledging to draw out your partner. Examples of ways to invite include the following:

"Tell me more."

"Say more about that."

"I'd like to hear more about what you are saying."

"What else can you tell me?"

"Is there anything more you want me to know?"

"I'd like to hear anything else you think I should know."

Notice that an invitation can take the form of a gentle command, a statement, or a question. In effect, you encourage the talker to tell you anything he or she wishes.

Invite after a pause. When others tell you their stories, they often pause, looking for your response. Most people unconsciously test listeners with brief pauses to see if it is okay to continue talking. They do not tell what they are really thinking, feeling, or wanting unless they are sure the listener wants to know what is going on inside of them. But many listeners take the pause as a cue to jump in and start directing the conversation by giving advice or asking questions. Do not do this. Instead, invite your partner to tell you more, and he or she will lead you to more useful information. You will understand your partner better.

Invite (time #1)

"Tell me more."

Invite again (time #2, time #3, and so on)

"Is there anything more you can tell me?"

"Is there anything else you want me to know?"

An invitation to continue is a very powerful message. In effect, it says to the person talking: "What you are saying is important to me. I have time to listen. Keep talking."

Often at the third or forth invitation, a person will say to you, "I don't know if this has anything to do with the situation or not, *but* . . ." What follows the "but" is usually gold! This is because you have demonstrated enough interest that he or she now has the trust and courage to say what is really on his or her mind. At this point, the person will usually give you core information.

Continue inviting until your partner says something to the effect: "I don't think there's anything more I can say about the situation," and in fact has nothing more to add. (And you will see congruent nonverbals indicating that is all.) At this point you will realize you have heard his or her full story.

Invite rather than direct or react. When you feel the urge to begin directing a conversation, do not do it. Instead, invite and see what happens next. You may be surprised at the important information you discover and may have cut off otherwise.

4. SUMMARIZE to Ensure Accuracy

The skill of summarizing helps ensure the accuracy of your understanding of your partner. Using it lets you both know that, in essence, you share the meaning of his or her message. Rather than say to your partner, "I understand what you are saying" (which can sound slightly arrogant and may be untrue), summarize his or her message to *demonstrate* that you accurately understand.

Have you ever found yourself in a situation where you and your partner sincerely agreed to something only to learn later that what you had agreed to was not the same as what he or she had? Or have you ever been in a tense discussion only to discover finally that the two of you were talking past each other? In each instance, you were victims of "unshared meanings."

Many misunderstandings have nothing to do with limited intelligence or lack of good will. Communication is complex and many factors contribute to misunderstandings. You say something, and your partner internally *embellishes* the message a bit, putting more into your message than you mean or intend. You may do the same with your partner's message.

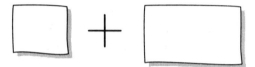

Or the reverse happens: You say something to your partner and he or she internally *reduces* your message to less than what you mean or intend. You may do this, too, with what your partner says.

When you understand what your partner says exactly as he or she intends, you both share a meaning.

A *shared meaning* occurs when the message sent by one person is the same as the message received by the other. Summarizing helps this occur.

To summarize, do the following:

- Repeat, in your own words, what you have just heard to be your partner's points. (Be complete, yet do not add to or subtract from the original message.)

- Ask your partner for confirmation or clarification of your summary.

It is most helpful to preface your summary with a statement that indicates your intention to summarize. For example, begin by saying, "I'd like to run back what you've just told me to be sure I've got it." Then you could continue with something such as, "You said you are feeling frustrated about . . . . Is that it?"

If your summary is accurate, you will see your partner respond positively. Usually there is a nod of the head or a smile indicating you are accurate. This really builds a relationship.

If you see that your summary is inaccurate, ask your partner to clarify. Then recycle the summary with the information just clarified. Sometimes it may be necessary to replay the summary a couple of times until both of you are satisfied that the message sent equals the message received.

As you summarize, include as many parts of the Awareness Wheel as your partner discloses.

Although this section focuses on the listener as the initiator of the summary, the partner talking can initiate a summary from the listener, too. For example, the talker can say, "I'd like to know what you've understood me to say, because this is important to me. Okay?"

5. ASK Open Questions

As you listen to your partner talk about an issue, you will notice parts of his or her story fall naturally into different zones of the Awareness Wheel. But even after you have attended carefully, acknowledged, invited your partner to say more, and summarized, you may still want additional specific information.

Ask open questions to gather or fill in missing information. Use the Awareness Wheel and the skill of asking open questions to help you gather information. Open questions often begin with a "W" word: Who, What, Where, and When; or How. (See the graphic on the next page for how to use open questions with the Awareness Wheel.)

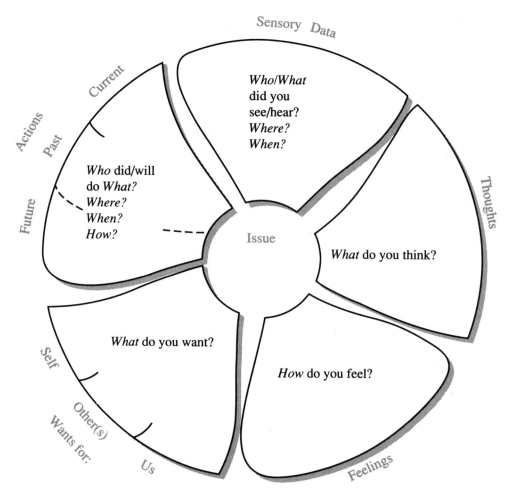

Open questions are the most effective kinds of questions. They give others more choice in how to answer. If you do not use a challenging tone, others will be free to answer the questions by describing their experiences in their own words.

In contrast, closed, narrow, or leading questions limit or attempt to direct responses. Examples of closed questions include:

- "Are you mad or sad?" (This requires an either-or response.)

- "Do you want to stop now?" (This requires a yes or no response.)

Ask open questions to clarify unclear/confusing sensory data. Even if you know your partner well enough to interpret certain private signs — a frown, a shrug of the shoulders, a particular facial expression — judging nonverbal behavior can be risky. You may not be accurate in what you think a nonverbal behavior means, so check it out — with an open question. For example:

> "I notice you are frowning (sensory data). What's up (open question)?"

Check out the accuracy of acknowledgments/thoughts. If you are not sure whether an acknowledgement or interpretation you have made is accurate, check it out with an open question.

> "You sound really angry with me (acknowledgment). How are you feeling (open question)?"

Ask open questions to clarify conflicting/indirect/mixed messages. When what you see does not match what you hear, comment on the incongruence, and ask a question to clarify the discrepancy. For example:

> "I know you said you would go sailing with me on Friday (sensory data), but you look like your heart isn't in it (interpretation). What do you really want to do (open question)?"

Avoid "Why" Questions

Pause for a moment and recall the last time someone asked you a "why" question. For example, "Why did you do that?" or "Why do you think that?" Do you recall feeling tense or on the spot? If so, this is a typical reaction to "why" questions.

"Why" questions usually disguise statements. The tone of voice accompanying them is often negative. "Why" questions can have the impact of challenging, blaming, and calling upon you to justify or defend your actions or position. They tend to put people on the defensive and increase resistance. Furthermore, you can seldom give a satisfactory answer to a "why" question, because the intent of most "why" questions is not to gain information but to persuade. For example:

"Why" Question	*Disguised Statement*
"Why don't you want to do it my way?"	"I want you to do it my way."

When you really want to make a statement, speak for self, and use your Awareness Wheel.

Advantages of Asking Questions

Asking open questions can be a powerful way to connect with your partner. Asking can capture masked expressions of feelings or unstated wants that he or she does not disclose directly. It can also help your partner become aware of hidden parts of his or her Awareness Wheel. Using the skill can bring clearer understanding between you.

Questions are also useful to structure an exchange when you want to focus information, for example, when a person talks too little or too much.

Limitations of Asking Questions

Some people mistakenly believe that good listening mainly involves asking questions. To demonstrate their interest in the talker's story, these listeners ask many questions. However, questions, even open questions, can interfere with effective listening for these reasons:

- Control of the story can easily shift from the person talking to the one listening. The listener's questions start to direct the story.

- Questions interfere with the natural flow of a talker's story. When you raise a question, the talker has to stop and think about what you asked. As a result, the talker may be led away or distracted from what he or she wants to say.

If given the chance, most people can tell their story best without prompting questions.

> Quality listening means
> getting the whole story accurately, the first time.

THE LISTENING CYCLE

While each of the five listening skills can be used independently and in any order as you listen, following a pattern for using the skills will maximize your listening effectiveness. The pattern is particularly helpful when the issue being discussed is *stressful or complex*.

The goal of listening with care is to help your partner tell his or her story as spontaneously and completely as possible. To accomplish this, apply the Listening Cycle.

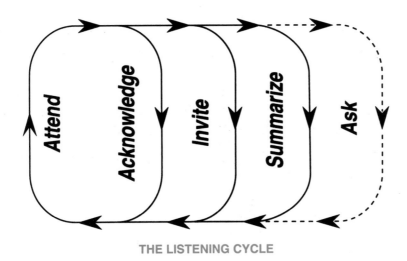

THE LISTENING CYCLE

Notice, in the Listening Cycle, the heavy lines circulating among Attend, Acknowledge, Invite, and Summarize. Recycling these skills, in any order, allows and encourages your partner to keep talking about the issue as spontaneously and completely as possible, with the most accuracy and the least influence or interference from you.

The Listening Cycle intentionally places Ask (open questions) last. Once your partner has told the story and has no more to add, then it is helpful to ask open questions to fill in missing information or to clarify parts of the issue.

History
own agendas
outside stress

Why Couples Hesitate to Listen to Each Other

As a listener, you can do a great deal either to hinder or to help your partner make a point. Several reasons why you may hesitate to let your partner "take the lead" and tell his or her story include:

- Perception that time is short

- Belief that your view of an issue will be overlooked by focusing initially on your partner's experience

- Concern that your partner will mistake your willingness to understand for agreement with what he or she is saying

- Fear that some information will be discovered that you will not know how to handle

- Recognition that you might have to change your perspective or behavior

- Apprehension that if you really listen to your partner, you will lose control over him, her, or the situation

The Benefits of Attentive Listening

When partners do not let issues build up but are responsive to each other's concerns as they develop, most people can express their concerns (issues) effectively within two to four minutes. This occurs if each partner simply listens attentively and does not react or interfere when the other talks.

When you use the Listening Cycle, you set your own concerns aside temporarily; you allow and encourage your partner to express his or her concerns fully. When you do this, you are more likely to:

- Get to the core of issues faster with less interpersonal stress.

- Gain uncontaminated, quality information.

- Encourage continued disclosure.

- Reduce fear and defensiveness — your own and your partner's — and increase trust and disclosure.

- Relate more constructively, when it is your turn to talk, to your partner's legitimate concerns.

- Earn the right to be heard after you have listened to your partner tell his or her full story.

- Save time later by not having to return to issues to clarify misunderstandings and mop up poor decisions.

- Create a collaborative atmosphere for generating new agreements based on current understanding.

- Leave your partner feeling good about both of you, which nurtures intimacy.

- Feel good about your own caring behavior.

REACTIVE LISTENING

Instructions: Use the space below to record your observations of the interaction between the talker and listener. Note the listener's verbal and nonverbal behavior and its impact on the talker's response.

Listener's Behavior:
Verbal/Nonverbal

Talker's Response:
Verbal/Nonverbal

OBSERVING/COACHING THE SKILL OF ATTENDING

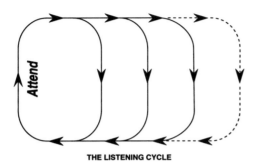

THE LISTENING CYCLE

Instructions: Use the graphic below to observe and coach the listener, who steps about the Awareness Wheel skills mat, as he or she tracks the talker's zones.

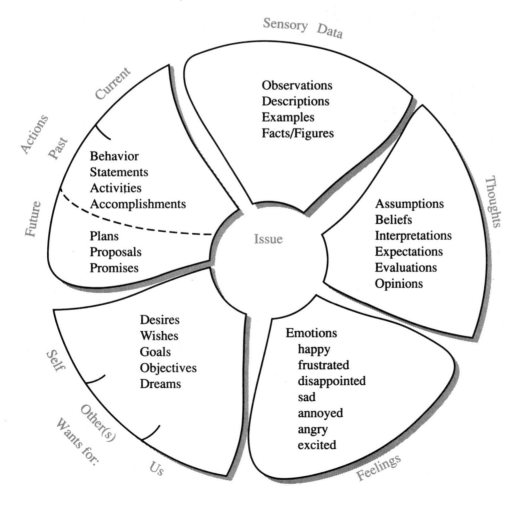

OBSERVING/COACHING THE SKILLS OF ACKNOWLEDGING AND INVITING

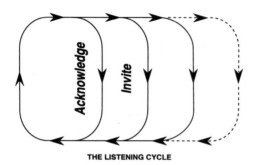

THE LISTENING CYCLE

Instructions: In the space below, note the listener's acknowledgments and invitations, and the talker's responses. If appropriate, coach the listener to acknowledge or invite more frequently (actively). If the listener strays into asking specific questions, redirect him or her back into acknowledging or inviting.

Listener's Behavior: **Talker's Response:**

Acknowledging
Other's Experience

Inviting
More Information

OBSERVING/COACHING THE SKILL OF SUMMARIZING

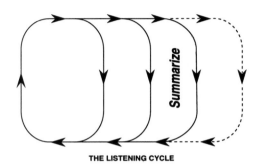

THE LISTENING CYCLE

Instructions: In the space below, note the listener's summarizing. As the listener summarizes, watch the talker's head. To what extent does he or she nod and smile indicating recognition of accuracy? Coach the listener to recycle the summary, if necessary, until the talker confirms the completeness and accuracy of the summary.

Listener's Behavior: **Talker's Response:**

Summarizing
to Ensure Accuracy

Combination of
Summarizing and Inviting

Other Listening Skills

LISTENING SKILLS ACTION PLAN

Instructions: Here is a list of the listening skills taught in Chapter 2. Complete the following steps:

Step 1. Without consulting your partner, mark each item with an "X" to represent your current use of each listening skill.

When you are with your partner, how often do you:	**Seldom**					**Often**
1. Attend — look, listen, track?	1	2	3	4	5	6
2. Acknowledge his or her experience?	1	2	3	4	5	6
3. Invite more information?	1	2	3	4	5	6
4. Summarize to ensure accuracy?	1	2	3	4	5	6
5. Ask open questions?	1	2	3	4	5	6

Step 2. Choose and list one or two skills to practice between now and the next session.

Skill: _____

Skill: _____

Step 3. Compare your choices with your partner's, and talk about where and when each of you will practice using the skills.

Between Sessions

Step 4. When you notice your partner using the listening skill(s) between sessions, give him or her some positive feedback. Encourage your partner by telling how his or her use of the skill(s) makes it easier for you to tell your story accurately.

LISTENING TO YOUR PARTNER — USING THE LISTENING CYCLE SKILLS MAT

Invite your partner to talk about something he or she would really like you to hear. (Your partner may wish to prepare by filling out an Awareness Wheel, but that is optional.)

Directions

1. Schedule a time and place for you to practice your listening skills with your partner.

2. Start by standing on the Listening Cycle skills mat with the "Listening Cycle" words facing you at your feet. (Be sure the mat does not slip on the floor when you step on it.) Your partner may or may not use the Awareness Wheel skills mat.

3. *Follow your partner to gain complete and accurate understanding* of what he or she is telling you — the main purpose of this exercise. Use the skills mat to apply and re-cycle these skills:

   - Attend

   - Acknowledge (especially feelings and wants)

   - Invite

   - Summarize

4. As your partner talks, avoid listening reactively by:

   - Disagreeing/objecting

   - Correcting

   - Advising

5. Ask open questions last, and do so only after you have gained your partner's confirmation that you have completely and accurately understood what he or she has told you.

6. Ask your partner, when you complete the exercise, how well he or she thinks you listened on a scale from low to high (1 2 3 4 5 6). If your score is lower than expected, ask for feedback and coaching to improve your rating.

APPLYING LISTENING SKILLS WITH KIDS

Consider using the listening skills when your child or adolescent wants to talk about —
or request — something that you would typically immediately respond to in a negative
way.

Directions

1. Decide if you wish to use the skills:

   Without the mat   *With the mat*
   (You may not want to let   (You may want the child to know that
   the child know as yet that   you are trying to improve communication
   you are trying the skills.)   and will use the mat as a help.)

2. In either case, be clear about the skills and the sequence of the Listening Cycle:

   • Attend

   • Acknowledge

   • Invite

   • Summarize

   • Ask

3. Reflect, afterwards, on:

   • the level of tension;

   • any mood shifts;

   • the outcome.

4. Consider how this is similar to or differs from your usual conversations in such
   situations with this child.

LISTENING SITUATIONS

Instructions: During the next week, practice your listening skills at home, work, and elsewhere. Use the space below to record your experiences with specific listening skills.

Situation   Skills   Outcome

Situation   Skills   Outcome

Situation   Skills   Outcome

Situation   Skills   Outcome

CLOSED VERSUS OPEN QUESTIONS

Closed questions limit a response. Open questions give the responder more options.

Instructions: The questions below are closed questions that refer to various zones of the Awareness Wheel. Change each closed question into an open question, tapping the same zone of the Wheel. Compare your changes with ours, at the bottom of the page.

1. Are you angry about what he said?

2. Did you see a smirk on her face?

3. Did you hear a snarl in his voice?

4. Will that make you glad or sad?

5. Did you call her back immediately?

6. Do you want to change jobs?

7. Is your plan all set now?

8. Will you return on Saturday or Sunday?

9. Do you think that's right or wrong?

10. Do you want to go or to stay?

Here are possible open questions to replace the closed ones above.

1. How are you feeling about what he said?

2. What kind of expression did you see on her face?

3. How was the tone of his voice?

4. How do you think you will feel about that?

5. When did you call her back?

6. What do you want to do about your job?

7. How are your plans coming?

8. When will you return?

9. What do you think about that?

10. What do you want to do?

REPLAY OF A RECENT CONVERSATION

Instructions: Recall a recent conversation you had with another person at home or work, in which you consciously used the talking and listening skills.

Use the Awareness Wheel below to recall what information you clearly disclosed.

Now, use the Awareness Wheel below to recall what information you helped the other person disclose, by using listening skills.

Reflect on the gains you have made in using the talking and listening skills.

ACTIONS FOR CARING ABOUT YOUR PARTNER

How have you been caring and not caring about your partner physically, emotionally, relationally, and spiritually over the past week?

Instructions: Use the space below to make notes about what (actions) you have been doing in each of these areas.

	Caring	**Not Caring**
Physically		
Emotionally		
Relationally		
Spiritually		

REVIEW YOUR ACTION PLAN AND LEARNING GOALS

How are you doing with your Chapter 2 Action Plan (see page 72) and your overall Learning Goals (see page 12)? How do these fit with caring about your partner? Be sure you are putting your plans and goals to work for you and your partner.

RESOLVING CONFLICTS
—
MAPPING ISSUES

3
Resolving Conflicts: Mapping Issues

Each person's experience — sensory data, thoughts, feelings, wants, and actions — is different and unique. Because this is so, partners often find that the potential exists for conflict in any event or situation that arises.

Conflict can have its root in any zone of the Awareness Wheel:

- Differing perceptions of sensory data
- Opposing beliefs, interpretations, expectations, values
- Disturbing feelings
- Competing wants and interests
- Offending behaviors

Outcome Results from Process

The way you and your partner make decisions about issues reveals the caring or uncaring attitudes — at least for the moment — you both hold toward one another. Likewise, how you talk and listen together about your separate awarenesses influences the quality of decisions you make and your satisfaction regarding them. And the way you handle your conflicts often strengthens or damages (emotionally or even physically) one another and your relationship.

In this chapter we will describe the processes people use to resolve their disagreements. You and your partner may find that you show a typical pattern in the way you handle your conflicts (regardless of the type of issue) and in the resulting outcomes to them. We will recommend a particular process, called Mapping an Issue, for satisfactorily resolving conflicts.

Outcome Possibilities

Once a conflict arises between partners, it moves toward some sort of outcome. Three possible outcomes to a conflict include the following: disappearance; impasse; or resolution.

Disappearance: The issue triggering the conflict goes away by itself as time passes.

Impasse: Partners get stuck and take no action. This may include agreeing to live with indecision temporarily, agreeing to disagree longer term, or reaching a real polarized standoff.

Resolution: Partners take action to reach closure on the conflict.

PROCESSES OF CONFLICT RESOLUTION

Before reaching any of the outcomes however, partners go through a process of attempting to deal with the issue. How they do this usually falls into one of five ways: avoid; persuade (fight or capitulate); float; compromise; or collaborate.

AVOID

When an issue with potential conflict occurs, some partners try to smooth it over with chitchat, skirt around it, or change the subject altogether. In an attempt to avoid conflict, they try to ignore or even deny the significance of the issue.

When partners use this process, decisions surrounding the issue are left to chance or happen by default. They hope the situation will go away, or they live with indecision. In the short run, this process may seem to work. But, in the long run and depending upon who has most at stake in the issue, this process can be dissatisfying.

PERSUADE

Sometimes partners attempt to persuade one another about how they each think the issue should be handled. One partner may sell or persuade to a stronger degree and the other person eventually complies. This approach can bring resolution to the issue, but negative feelings between the two partners often result.

Fight or Capitulate

If neither partner gives in, the disagreement can escalate into a strong argument or destructive fight. The conflict may result in an impasse. Or, if one partner capitulates feeling angry and resentful, he or she may withdraw, and, with snide remarks or other underhanded behaviors, actually continue the conflict under the surface.

Even if a resolution is reached, these fighting and capitulating processes are not satisfying and can be damaging to the relationship. While one partner appears to win, in the long term, both lose.

FLOAT

With this process, partners discuss and search for solutions, but never find answers. Nothing is brought to closure. During their discussions, they skim the surface of an issue, never really embracing their full awarenesses or committing themselves to congruent action to resolve the issue. They may even agree to live with indecision, which continues indefinitely. The result is endless talk and no action.

While dealing with issues in this way may seem to be safe, in the long run, the inaction is dissatisfying.

COMPROMISE

Another alternative for resolving conflicts is to compromise — reach a solution through tradeoffs. Here, partners figure out and willingly exchange concessions of differing importance to one another. Each gives something to get something; each gains and loses something. While neither person gets everything he or she wants, both get something.

The resolution may work, yet may or may not be fully satisfactory to both.

COLLABORATE

This process goes beyond compromise. In the process of collaborating, each partner seeks to find or generate a solution to an issue that will benefit both of them. To do this, both partners tune into and disclose their full awarenesses to understand their conflict and to create a mutually workable solution. They show attitudes of I-care-about-me and I-care-about-you, and the process brings action.

Collaborative agreements are built on understanding and consensus, so they may take more time initially to achieve. However, the results are more satisfying, and the "both-win" decisions generally strengthen the relationship. Furthermore, collaborative processes actually save time and energy in the long run because they prevent the accumulative fall-out of poor or partial initial decisions. *Talking and Listening Together* teaches concepts and skills for collaboration.

Process and Outcome Patterns

Any process can produce any outcome. However, a certain process tends to yield a specific outcome more frequently. The combination of the process and the outcome of a conflict forms a particular pattern, and various patterns usually result in differing levels of satisfaction.

Look at the conflict resolution processes and the outcomes in the following chart and think about what might be typical for you and your partner. Then consider your own level of satisfaction with your usual pattern.

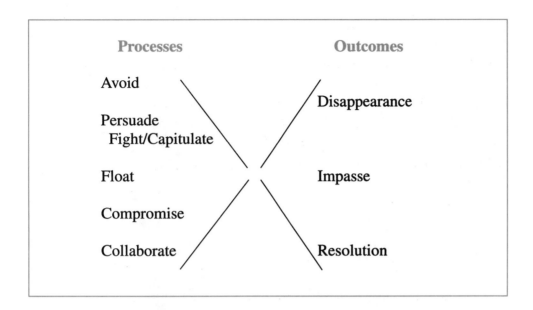

	Processes		Outcomes
	Avoid		Disappearance
	Persuade		
	Fight/Capitulate		
	Float		Impasse
	Compromise		
	Collaborate		Resolution

MAPPING ISSUES:
RESOLVING CONFLICTS COLLABORATIVELY

When you and your partner have a difficult situation to handle, you can resolve it by Mapping the Issue. This Mapping process is a structured way to apply I-care-about-me and I-care-about-you attitudes in your behaviors as you face conflict. It is a *collaborative process* that takes into account all zones in the Awareness Wheel to help you reach the *most satisfying resolution*. To Map an Issue, you:

Step 1. Identify and Define the Issue

Step 2. Contract to Work Through the Issue

Step 3. Understand the Issue Completely

Step 4. Identify Wants

Step 5. Generate Options

Step 6. Choose Actions

Step 7. Test the Action Plan

Step 8. Evaluate the Outcome

When to Map an Issue

Since the process for Mapping an Issue takes time and is thorough, you use it selectively for issues that arise between you and your partner. Once you are familiar with the process, you will find it to be a good guide in any discussion through uncharted or rough territory. Consider Mapping the Issue when you:

- think the issue is *important or complicated*

- experience considerable *tension and conflict*

- want *maximum input* from one another about the issue

- seek the *best solution* in the situation

STEP 1. IDENTIFY AND DEFINE THE ISSUE

Issues arise when there is some disruption in expectations — when there is a gap between what is *anticipated* and what is actually *experienced*. The *cue* to an issue can register in any awareness zone — sensing, thinking, feeling, wanting, or doing.

Either you or your partner, can first spot the issue and bring it to the other's attention. In Step 1, you ask:

- What is the issue?

The "what" is the issue itself. It can have a topical, personal, or relational focus.

- Whose issue is it?

Is the issue mine, yours, or ours?

To answer this, think about who is being affected and what is at stake for whom. Clarifying ownership of the issue is particularly useful, for example, when the issue is mine and does not involve you, but I would like you to consult with me (help me Map my Issue). For instance, the issue could be about a difficult situation at work or a stressful exchange with one of our children.

When you are clear about the issue — proceed to the next step.

STEP 2. CONTRACT TO WORK THROUGH THE ISSUE

Have you ever wanted to talk with your partner about something but found him or her unreceptive? When this happens, it is easy to feel resentment and to assume that your partner is not interested in your concern. Sometimes you may try to push harder to be heard despite all the verbal or nonverbal signs of unavailability.

Often it is not the issue, but rather it is a bad time or place for the other person to talk about your concern; in another situation, your partner may be very willing to talk.

Contracting — Setting Procedures

Rather than assuming a lack of interest or trying to force participation, consider another alternative — contracting. Contracting means checking your partner's *willingness and readiness* to work through a particular issue before launching into the issue. To do this, you *set procedures for conducting your discussion before starting the conversation.* Getting your partner's okay first demonstrates respect for one another and prevents useless frustration as well as waste of time and energy. The more fast-moving and complex your life is, the more intentional you have to be about contracting.

Consider eight elements as you set procedures — establish your informal contract. One element out of sync is all that is necessary to interfere with the process of working through an issue effectively.

Procedures	Who
	Where
	When
	How
	Energy
	Length
	Time Out
	Check the Process

From the descriptions below, consider how each one of the procedural elements influences issue resolution:

Who is included?

Deciding whose problem it is helps you set appropriate boundaries about who should and who should not be included in the actual discussion of the issue. Sometimes you and your spouse will prefer to talk privately without children or other persons present. Other times you will want certain people included in the discussion. Agree on who should or should not participate and hold the discussion when all players can meet.

Where can we talk?

Place is important. Choose a private place. Limit the telephone, television, and other distractions. Making critical decisions during a meal may not be the right place; it interferes with savoring your food. Likewise, heavy discussions in bed may be out of bounds; one partner drops off to sleep, while the other cannot get to sleep. You might want to take a walk, a drive in your car and park, or settle into a comfortable spot in your house. Find a good place that fits for both of you.

When can we talk?

Trying to force a discussion at the wrong time or giving an issue inadequate time only generates more tension and dissonance. On the other hand, when both partners are ready and want to deal with something, even in a limited time frame, you may be surprised at what can be accomplished.

Considering time also gives both of you a chance to prepare adequately for the discussion. Some folks prefer — and some situations require self-talk— time to reflect on awareness. For other people, postponing a conversation only creates anxiety about what will be said or what will happen. Consider the other person's preferences as well as your own and contract accordingly.

How will we talk?

Sometimes it is useful to agree on a process for Mapping an Issue. Decide if you want to:

- Use the skill mats

- Write and talk (see pair exercise, pages 106-109)

- Have an open discussion, including all steps of the process described here

Do we have *energy* available for dealing with the issue?

Even with all the other right conditions, occasionally physical or mental fatigue dominates. Often the solution to an issue is closely tied to the energy you can put into discussing it. Some issues are best reserved for a time when you both have the energy to handle them. However, chronically low energy may suggest you are avoiding an issue or some dimension of your awareness.

What *length* of time shall we talk?

You probably have had the experience of beginning a discussion and then at two or three o'clock in the morning (in the middle of an argument) asking yourself, "Why didn't we just stop at midnight and plan to take it up later?" Sometimes you may want to say ahead of time when you will stop. At that point, you can plan when to pick up the discussion again.

Either can *call time out* from the discussion.

Have a rule that either partner can call time out and stop the exchange. Without this safety valve, a discussion can simply go too long or angrily get out of hand. Then, when the time is right, recontract to discuss the issue further. Issues do not always need to be resolved at one sitting. Often, time to digest what has been heard or to cool off brings new perspective and resolution.

Either can *check the process* of the discussion.

Agree, that at any point, either you or you partner can request that you check the process. For instance, you might say, "I'd like to stop a moment and clarify what we're doing right now. Are we on Step 3 — Understanding the Issue Completely, or on Step 4 — Identifying Wants?" Or you might say, "I agreed to listen while you talked, yet I've been telling you what I heard. I think I'm a little off track."

Running down this list each time you want to deal with an issue is not always necessary. Be aware, however, that an underlying informal procedural contract runs through every discussion. Attend to the other person's nonverbals for clues to whether your contract to work on the issue is in effect or not. If in you are in doubt, check it out.

Setting procedures increases each person's involvement and puts you and your partner in charge of the exchange — the two of you establish your own rules. When you and your partner genuinely want to resolve an issue and agree on procedures for continuing, you have a good start on settling your conflict.

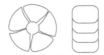

Illustration

Jack and Kay, two participants in a Couple Communication group, determined the following as their current issues:

Jack's issues included:

— Dealing with anger in our relationship

— Budgeting for Cathy's wedding

— Determining priorities for home improvements

— Considering a new car

Kay's issues were:

— Budgeting for the wedding

— Handling our anger

— Planning for vacation

— Fixing sliding glass door

After comparing their issues, they contracted (set procedures that fit for themselves) to map their common issue of handling anger. They would do this at home, first by writing individually and then by talking and listening to one another. They wrote "handling anger" at the center of their Awareness Wheels in each of their workbooks and proceeded to Step 3.

Issue:
Handling
Anger

STEP 3. UNDERSTAND THE ISSUE COMPLETELY

The purpose of this step is to develop complete understanding of the issue before taking action. This prevents pre-closure — jumping quickly to solutions that do not fit.

To understand the issue, each participant answers these four questions from his or her individual perspective:

- What have I done, or what am I currently doing, that is working or not working?
- What have I seen and heard?
- What do I think is going on?
- How am I feeling?

Then one person at a time uses the talking skills, while the other person applies the listening skills, to share awareness with one another. Take turns disclosing and using the Listening Cycle until you accurately understand each other's perspective. Clarify misunderstandings and feelings.

Understanding as the Solution

Occasionally you will discover that it is not necessary to go beyond Step 3, because the very process of understanding the issue in itself has become the solution. When this occurs, you and your partner will find that your external and internal information all fit together peacefully. You will experience a shift where understanding and knowing, not action, is the only solution necessary.

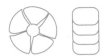

Illustration continued

Here's what Jack filled in for understanding the issue:

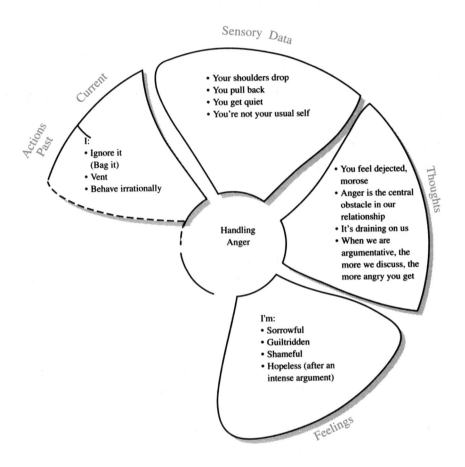

Kay's awareness consisted of the following:

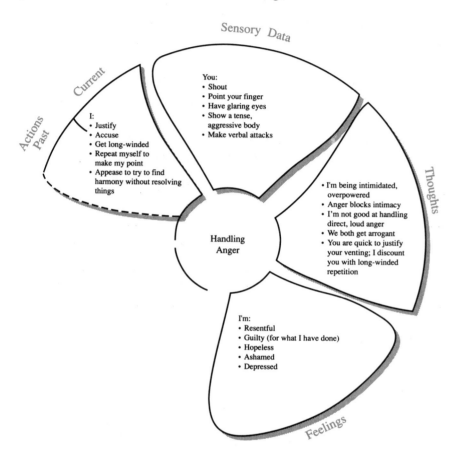

Sensory Data

Current

Actions Past

I:
• Justify
• Accuse
• Get long-winded
• Repeat myself to make my point
• Appease to try to find harmony without resolving things

You:
• Shout
• Point your finger
• Have glaring eyes
• Show a tense, aggressive body
• Make verbal attacks

Handling Anger

Thoughts

• I'm being intimidated, overpowered
• Anger blocks intimacy
• I'm not good at handling direct, loud anger
• We both get arrogant
• You are quick to justify your venting; I discount you with long-winded repetition

I'm:
• Resentful
• Guilty (for what I have done)
• Hopeless
• Ashamed
• Depressed

Feelings

STEP 4. IDENTIFY WANTS

Step 4 focuses on the wants — to *be*, to *do*, and to *have* — surrounding the issue. You might also consider things you do *not* want, if that is relevant.

Most importantly, be sure to consider everyone who has a stake in the issue. Do this by answering these three questions:

• What do I want *for me* regarding the issue?

• What do I want (positive) *for my partner?*

• What do I want for *us?*

When mapping an issue together, the first partner to share wants often may not be able to do so "for my partner," because he or she has not yet heard the partner's wants. Once both have had a chance to talk about "wants for me," then determining "wants for my partner" can be done more readily.

As you consider wants *for* your partner, think carefully about what you have heard your partner say about his or her interests and desires. If you can affirm your partner's wants, include them as your wants for him or her, too. (Be careful not to confuse what you want *for* your partner, with what you want *from* your partner. Put what you want *from* your partner under your wants for yourself.)

Be sure to include all of your wants. As you identify your wants, clarify what getting your desires would do for you. Consider the impact on the relationship system. Also do the same with wants for your partner.

Building on the wants of others is a critical element in resolving conflicts. Building on wants for the relationship is a system perspective that increases good will and a collaborative spirit.

Illustration continued

Jack's wants were:

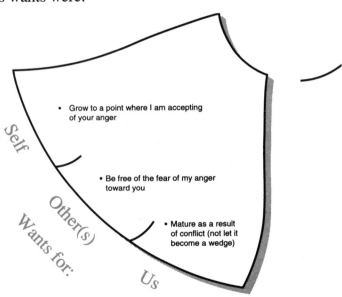

- Grow to a point where I am accepting of your anger

- Be free of the fear of my anger toward you

- Mature as a result of conflict (not let it become a wedge)

Self

Other(s)

Wants for:

Us

Kay's wants were:

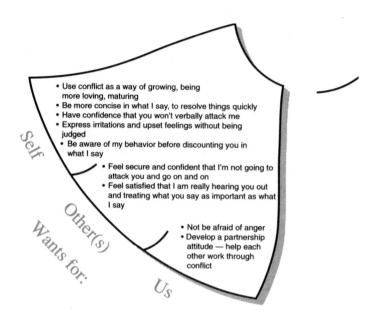

STEP 5. GENERATE OPTIONS

Now, based on your expanded understanding of the issue and any convergent wants between you and your partner, brainstorm what you could do to resolve the issue or at least move it ahead.

At this point, the question to answer is:

What *can I do* about the issue?

- For me

- For my partner

- For us

Think openly, small, and positively. Rather than trying to visualize one big solution, generate a diverse list of small positive actions you *can actually take* as a next step.

Consider every option possible. Be sure to include both new possibilities that have not been tried, as well as actions taken in the past that have been helpful. But do not keep doing what is not working.

Generate possibilities without pausing to critique the options. Choosing and evaluating the options are steps you will do later.

Sometimes you may find it useful to set your expectations for improvement in terms of a percentage figure. For example, if you could achieve twenty percent improvement in the situation as a next step, would that be satisfactory? Without really thinking about it, we often set an unrealistic (one hundred percent) expectation and then feel overwhelmed or discouraged when we try to bring about a gigantic solution.

Illustration continued

Jack was willing to consider these actions:

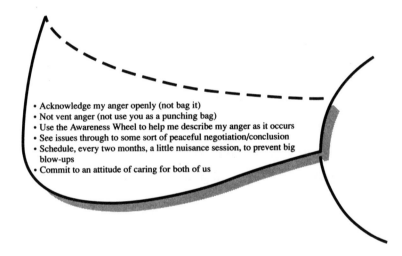

- Acknowledge my anger openly (not bag it)
- Not vent anger (not use you as a punching bag)
- Use the Awareness Wheel to help me describe my anger as it occurs
- See issues through to some sort of peaceful negotiation/conclusion
- Schedule, every two months, a little nuisance session, to prevent big blow-ups
- Commit to an attitude of caring for both of us

Kay was willing to consider the following:

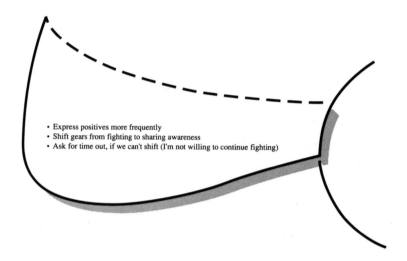

- Express positives more frequently
- Shift gears from fighting to sharing awareness
- Ask for time out, if we can't shift (I'm not willing to continue fighting)

STEP 6. CHOOSE ACTIONS

When you have generated possibilities, share them with your partner.

In choosing which actions to implement, consider:

- the worst and best things that could happen with each action

- the options that are the most workable

Synthesize and combine actions if you wish. At this point, the primary question for each partner to answer is:

What *will I commit* to doing?

- For me

- For my partner

- For us

Illustration continued

Here's what Jack committed to do:

ACTION PLAN

What I Will Do:

   For Me: Use Wheel to describe anger

   For Partner: Have I-care-about-you attitude

Kay chose these actions:

ACTION PLAN

What I Will Do:

   For Me: Shift gears to sharing awareness

   For Partner: Express more positives

If possible, set specific times and places to carry out the actions.

STEP 7. TEST THE ACTION PLAN

After you have chosen your action plan, test it. Pause for a moment, and each of you imagine yourself carrying out your future actions. Check the zones of your Wheel for fit. If each of you sees, hears, and experiences yourself following through with your behavior effectively, great! Your plan fits.

However, if either of you cannot carry out your action plan, consider what is interfering. Is it something you think, feel, or really do not want to do that is preventing the action? The belief, fear, or want in the zone of your Awareness Wheel in which you find yourself "stuck" becomes a new issue that is really blocking resolution of the original issue.

If time and energy are not available immediately to map and resolve the new issue, contract to deal with the new issue later.

Illustration continued

When Jack and Kay internally tested their action plans, Kay said, "I feel excited and relieved knowing we can improve this area of our relationship." Jack concurred and said, "Let's do it."

STEP 8. EVALUATE THE OUTCOME

After time passes and you have had a chance to act, you can evaluate your plan and consider whether or not your action is effective.

If your action is effective, you will feel something positive. When the outcome is pleasing, celebrate! Be sure to give your partner positive feedback for his or her contribution to the solution as well.

If your action is not effective, you may experience a range of negative feelings — disappointment, frustration, or embarrassment. When the outcome is not satisfactory, recycle your Awareness Wheel and come up with a different action plan. Do not keep repeating actions that do not work.

What Mapping Issues Does for You

Mapping Issues provides a comprehensive structure for resolving conflicts. It helps you to see where you are in the process of a discussion. It also helps you:

- **Recognize** your own contribution and response to a situation.
- **Keep** focus on the central issue.
- **Include** powerful feelings and wants.
- **Take** appropriate action based on full awareness.

For an important issue — for a couple, family, or work group — using this process incorporates communication concepts and skills to help you work through an issue collaboratively and effectively.

LIST OF CONFLICTS

Date _____

Instructions: Think of your concerns at home, at work, and elsewhere. As you reflect, write down a word or phrase to represent each issue involving conflict that comes into your mind.

Topical   **Personal**

Relational

When you have completed your list, turn back to the "List of Current Issues" you made earlier, on page 38. Compare issues at these two points in time. Which issues on the first list have been resolved or disappeared? If you wish, move any old issues to this new list.

PATTERNS OF CONFLICT RESOLUTION

Every couple has an informal, often unspoken agreement about how they go about resolving conflicts. Here are the lists of the conflict-resolution processes and the outcomes identified in Chapter 3.

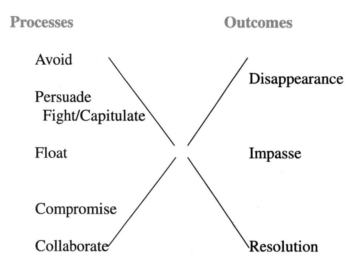

Processes   Outcomes

Avoid

Persuade
  Fight/Capitulate   Disappearance

Float   Impasse

Compromise

Collaborate   Resolution

Step 1. Use the *process/outcome* options listed above to identify, from your perspective, the most frequent conflict resolution patterns between you and your partner. Rate your satisfaction level with each pattern. (Do not consult your partner for this step.)

Process	Outcome	Satisfaction (Low, Medium, High)
1.		
2.		
3.		

Step 2. Compare and discuss, with your partner, the patterns you have identified with those he or she has identified.

OBSERVING/COACHING A COUPLE MAPPING AN ISSUE USING THE AWARENESS WHEEL AND LISTENING CYCLE SKILLS MATS

To Observe:

- Look for:

    Accuracy — the clear use of talking and listening skills

    Completeness — the completion of each mapping step

- Use the observation/coaching worksheet (see next page) to jot down notes (key words, phrases, gestures) for feedback later.

To Coach:

- Make sure partners rotate (take turns on the talking and listening skills mats) with each mapping step.

- Encourage accurate use of the talking skills.

- Encourage active use of the listening skills.

- Use the talking and listening skills to coach the process. Be cautious about suggesting issue insights or solutions. (Do not try to resolve the couple's issue for them.)

OBSERVING/COACHING A COUPLE MAPPING AN ISSUE USING THE SKILLS MATS

	Notes		(✔) Step
Mapping Steps	**Partner A**	**Partner B**	**Completed**

Step 1. Identify/Define the Issue

Step 2. Contract — Set Procedures

Step 3. Understand the Issue
              Completely

Step 4. Identify Wants

Step 5. Generate Options

Step 6. Choose Action(s)

Step 7. Test the Action Plan

Step 8. Evaluate the Outcome

(The couple can do
this step later.)

MAPPING ISSUES ACTION PLAN

Instructions: Rate yourself according to the items under each step below:

	Special Strength	Okay As Is	Work Area
Step 1. Identify and Define the Issue	_____	_____	_____
Step 2. Contract to Work Through the Issue	_____	_____	_____
Step 3. Understand the Issue Completely	_____	_____	_____
Step 4. Identify Wants	_____	_____	_____
Step 5. Generate Options	_____	_____	_____
Step 6. Choose Action(s)	_____	_____	_____
Step 7. Test the Action Plan	_____	_____	_____
Step 8. Evaluate the Outcome	_____	_____	_____

Choose one or two steps to improve.

	With Whom	Where	When	How
Step ____				
Step ____				

MAPPING AN ISSUE

Date: _____

STEP 1. IDENTIFY AND DEFINE THE ISSUE
(See Worksheet, "Updated List of Current Issues," Chapter 3, page 101)

- What is the issue?

- Whose issue is it?

STEP 2. CONTRACT TO WORK THROUGH THE ISSUE (Set Procedures)

Consider/check out procedures:

- *Who* is included?

- *Where* can we talk?

- *When* can we talk?

- *How* will we talk?

- Do we have the *energy* for dealing with the issue?

- How *long* will we talk?

- We agree that either one of us can:
  Call Time Out
  Check Process

Select a joint issue (an issue in common) which you and your partner want to work through. Write it in the hub of each of your Wheels (see graphic on the next page, Step 3).

STEP 3. UNDERSTAND THE ISSUE COMPLETELY

Fill in the partial Awareness Wheel below with words and short phrases which represent your awareness (experience) of the issue.

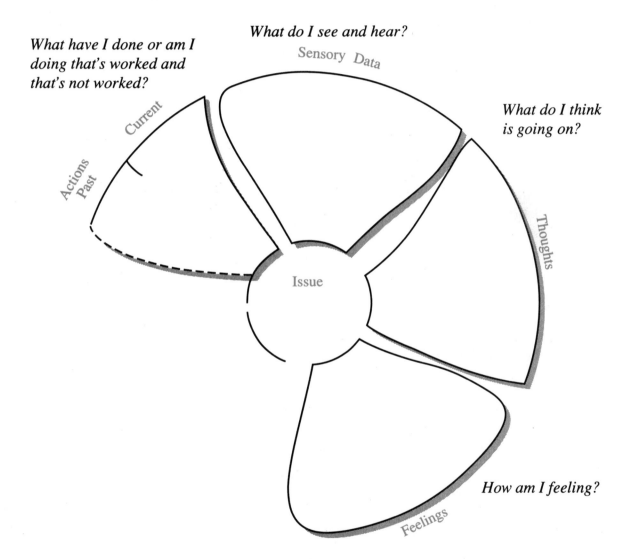

Share what you have written with your partner. (Each of you will be describing your experience of the same issue from your own perspective.)

STEP 4. IDENTIFY WANTS

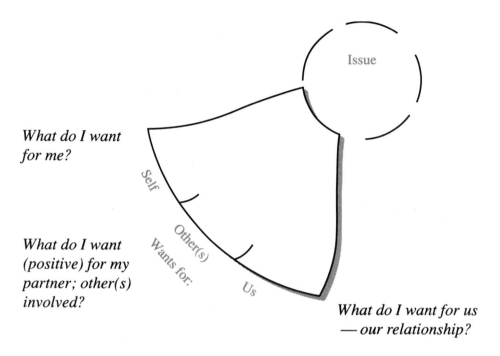

What do I want for me?

What do I want (positive) for my partner; other(s) involved?

What do I want for us — our relationship?

After you have filled out your wants, share and discuss them with your partner.

STEP 5. GENERATE OPTIONS

Based on all the information you have written and discussed, generate a list of actions that you would be willing to take to resolve the issue.

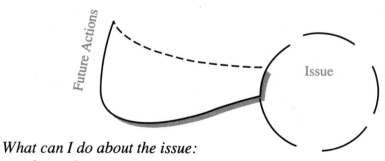

What can I do about the issue:
- *for me?*
- *for other(s)?*
- *for us?*

STEP 6. CHOOSE ACTION(S)

Decide which action(s) you will take. Record your "Action Steps."

Action Steps

What I Will Do	*By When*
_____	_____
_____	_____
_____	_____

STEP 7. TEST THE ACTION

After you have chosen your action step(s), test it. Pause for a moment, and visualize yourself actually carrying out each action at a specific time and place. If you find yourself actually following through with each action effectively, great! Your future action(s) "fits." If however, you find yourself unable to do the future action, consider what is blocking you. Is it something you think (believe about the issue), feel, or really do not want to do that interferes with taking action?

Share the test of your action with your partner.

If you or your partner are experiencing reservations about a future action, explore the hesitation and incorporate this awareness into a revised and realistic action plan.

STEP 8. EVALUATE THE OUTCOME

After you complete your action steps, in time, evaluate them. If the outcome is pleasing, celebrate. If it is not satisfactory, re-map the issue. In any event, do not repeat actions that do not work.

USING THE SKILLS MAT TO TEACH THE AWARENESS WHEEL TO YOUR FAMILY

Directions

1. Choose an issue, which is not too heavy, that involves all of your family members.

2. Set up a time when everyone can be together.

3. Introduce the family members to the Awareness Wheel by stepping around the skills mat, describing each zone of the Wheel.

4. Tell everyone to stand around the mat when you are ready to discuss the issue. Then one by one, in any order, let each member take turns using the mat to talk about his or her experience of the issue.

5. Apply (since you have already learned the skills) the listening skills to be sure everyone is accurately and completely heard. (Do some gentle coaching, if necessary.)

6. Talk about the issue until you as a family discover a satisfactory future action, gain new understanding, or call time out.

CHOOSING COMMUNICATION STYLES

4

Choosing Communication Styles: Ways of Talking and Listening

Each time you say something, your message contains two parts: *what* you say — the content, and *how* you say it — the style. Both parts influence how your message is received, yet people often think that they change the nature of their conversations simply by shifting the content, for example, from sports to friends.

While changing what you talk about has an impact, your messages are changed mostly by shifting style — how you talk about something. Your verbal and nonverbal style is a command message. It tells others how to take your message about the content — whether you are joking, angry, pleased, or serious.

Likewise, you can vary your style of listening. How you listen has a measurable effect on the quality of information the other person expresses.

Since people respond to *how* as much as they do to *what,* the outcome of a conversation varies dramatically depending on the talking and listening styles you use in the process. The way you talk and listen either helps or interferes with the conversation process. Your style also demonstrates the uncaring or caring attitudes you hold toward yourself and your partner. Many failures to communicate stem from the use of styles of communication inappropriate for the situation.

STYLES OF COMMUNICATION

How you talk to someone falls into one of four major communication-style categories, and *how you listen* to someone also falls into one of the four categories. The Communication Styles Map shows these various categories. In the map, each of the talking styles corresponds with a listening style.

Each style has typical behaviors associated with it that have a predictable impact upon a conversation. Using the talking and listening skills can give you more flexibility to converse in a particular style.

Go Through The 4 styles... then teach "Straight talk"

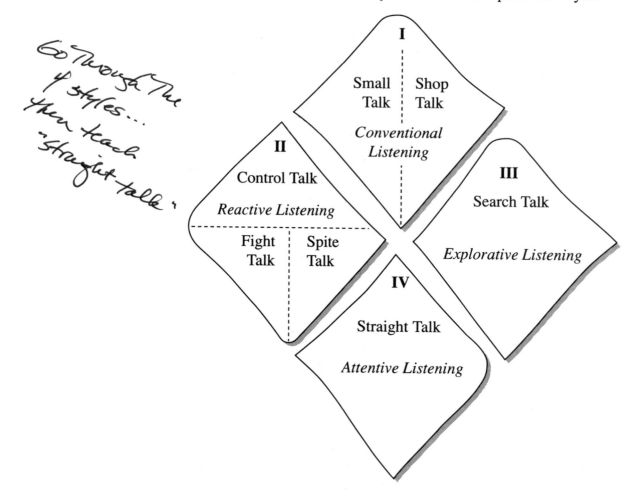

STYLE I

SMALL TALK AND SHOP TALK
CONVENTIONAL LISTENING

Small Talk, Shop Talk, and Conventional Listening are forms of the sociable styles people use most often to maintain the status quo and exchange routine information. The content is ordinary, everyday fare.

SMALL TALK

This friendly, common, and sometimes playful style keeps the world going around smoothly. When you want to relax or keep things moving in an easy and light way, you probably use Small Talk. It is the way you move in and out of conversations — in person or on the phone — with your partner, family, friends, boss, customers, clients, and strangers.

In Small Talk, your intentions are to be pleasant, find out how the other person is, and not rock the boat. Conversations usually revolve around the weather, news, sports, daily routines, family, special events, and other topics of general interest.

Typical Small Talk Behaviors

Hellos and good-byes: "How are you doing today?" "See you later."

Passing the time: "Who do you think will win the election?"

Storytelling: "You wouldn't believe what happened to me last night. As I got into my car . . . ."

Non-hostile joking: "You're not a very good influence on me."

Catching up: "What did you do today?"

Sharing events of the day: "Michael called from Germany today. He said Claudia had her baby. It's a girl."

Discussing biographical data, personal traits, habits, health, appearances: "I grew up in Denver"; "You have a quick wit"; "I seldom miss breakfast"; "My shoulder has been sore lately"; "You're missing a button."

Impact of Small Talk

Small Talk conversations with your partner or other family members demonstrate the basic care you feel for one another. As you take time to chitchat and share events of each other's day, you show evidence of your mutual affection and enjoyment of one another without saying directly, "I like you; I enjoy being with you."

In the busy world many of us live in, Small Talk provides relaxing and refreshing time together. And while a good joke may reduce tension, it is very difficult to have a free and nurturing Small Talk conversation with another person when you are feeling tension about an unresolved issue with that person.

SHOP TALK

Shop Talk is essential for carrying on most everyday activities. In Shop Talk you focus on task-related matters — maintaining and generating information to get a job done. During an average day, you probably have many Shop Talk exchanges at home and at work.

Typical Shop Talk Behaviors

Reporting: "Susan's throat culture was negative."

Providing facts: "The dentist raised his rates by ten percent."

Checking up: "When will the painter be finished?"

Scheduling: "How about having lunch together tomorrow?"

Following up: "Bob, did you turn the water off in the front yard?"

Making routine decisions: "John will feed the dog. I'll load the car, while you close up the house."

Passing on messages: "Your dad called and said he'd pick up the photos on his way home."

Impact of Shop Talk

While Small Talk keeps relationships on the light side, Shop Talk manages the routines in a system by planning, coordinating and maintaining tasks and events.

CONVENTIONAL LISTENING

When you want to make contact with others, and be available in a pleasant, sociable way, you listen conventionally. In doing so, you serve as a relaxed sounding board for whatever the speaker offers. You are generally interested in and usually agreeable with the conversation content, but you do not expend much energy in the process.

While you might be fully involved, your responses help keep talking on a light level, usually in Small Talk or Shop Talk. At other times, your interest may be limited, so you listen "with one ear only."

Typical Conventional Listening Behaviors:

Partial attending

Varying eye contact

Casual acknowledgments

Calm body movements

Allowable interruptions

Impact of Conventional Listening

Hearing other people's experiences and stories can be fun and refreshing. Conventional Listening also keeps you informed about routine matters. While the style offers a way to be together with your partner comfortably, your emotional involvement is limited — sometimes even superficial — as you maintain some distance. Conventional Listening is not an intimate style of listening.

If you are listening in a halfhearted manner, and your partner is wanting more responsiveness and involvement from you, Conventional Listening can trigger annoyance or even anger. On the other hand, if you have not had much time with your partner, and you are feeling out of touch, a Small Talk and Conventional Listening conversation can be stimulating.

In any event, when there are important, nonroutine issues to discuss, this style is too limited and disengaged to help you and your partner get to the heart of the matter.

STYLE I COMMUNICATION

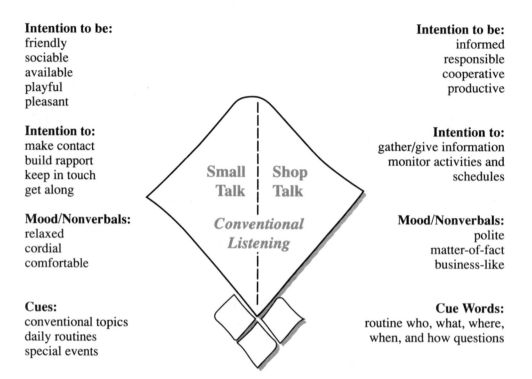

Intention to be:
friendly
sociable
available
playful
pleasant

Intention to:
make contact
build rapport
keep in touch
get along

Mood/Nonverbals:
relaxed
cordial
comfortable

Cues:
conventional topics
daily routines
special events

Intention to be:
informed
responsible
cooperative
productive

Intention to:
gather/give information
monitor activities and
schedules

Mood/Nonverbals:
polite
matter-of-fact
business-like

Cue Words:
routine who, what, where,
when, and how questions

(Diagram labels: Small Talk | Shop Talk — *Conventional Listening*)

STYLE II

CONTROL TALK, FIGHT TALK, AND SPITE TALK
REACTIVE LISTENING

Style II, through power and control, aims at gaining agreement or compliance, or it attempts to resist change. When using this style, you strive for a certain outcome, even if it has to be forced. You focus always on the other person — not yourself — trying to get him or her to "buy in" or "shape up." This is true whether you are talking or listening.

In three different ways of talking in Style II, people try to exert their power. The first way — Control Talk — sends messages intended to be constructive. The other two — Fight Talk and Spite Talk — send negative, potentially destructive messages. Most of the statements revolve around thoughts (who or what is right or wrong) and actions (what your partner should or should not do) on the Awareness Wheel.

CONTROL TALK

When you want to direct, advise, or persuade, Control Talk is a natural style to use. Most selling, directing, bargaining, supervising, teaching, advocating, and preaching activities go on in Control Talk.

Typical Control Talk Behaviors

Directing: "Call the garage and tell them you need the car by one-thirty."

Evaluating: "This procedure is twice as good as the old way."

Setting expectations, establishing boundaries: "You understand, don't you, that you need to be back here by nine o'clock, or we'll go without you?"

Advising/prescribing solutions: "You have to take your time with Max. You can't push him. Here's how to handle him . . . ."

Cautioning/warning: "Be careful when you lift that box. The bottom is weak."

Closed/directive questions: "Don't you think that . . . ?" "Wouldn't you agree that . . . ?"

Advocating/selling: "Just try it once. If you don't like it, I won't say anything more."

Assuming/speaking for others: "We're all morning people and could meet at seven a.m."

Praising: "You look great in your new blue suit."

Impact of Control Talk

Control Talk is the take-charge talking style, proactive, and efficient. When it works, others agree and comply with your directives. In its brevity and efficiency, however, it can create misunderstanding, distance, and tension.

Most people accept direction when it is useful. In fact, families become anxious and disorganized when parents are not in charge. However, people like to exchange information and participate in making decisions which affect them; no one likes to be ordered around. So when Control Talk is the main style used, it breeds resistance and resentment which usually slides into Fight or Spite Talk.

For example, "Tell Joe he should cut the grass," may sound like a routine directive. But that may not be the case if a remarried couple is stuck in a battle over whose child is favored for a particular activity. Then this otherwise innocent directive may set off a retort: "Don't you tell me what to have my son do! You can't even get your own daughter out of bed in the morning."

Excessive use of Control Talk between you and your partner can indicate you are experiencing mounting pressures in your lives. Too much of the style might even suggest you are heading for an explosion in Fight Talk. However, recognizing that this style signals tension allows you to view it as an early warning sign of distress in your relationship. Then you can determine to shift to a more self- and other-nurturing style.

FIGHT TALK

Fight Talk attempts to force change. As you verbally push and pull, your negative emotions run high. Your tone of voice and choice of words signal frustration, anger, and tension. Language is direct, aggressive, and often punitive.

Fight Talk is a reactive, rather than a proactive, style of communication. Fight Talk usually erupts around unclear or disrupted expectations — a change in plans, shortage of time, money, or energy — when people feel fearful, angry, threatened, desperate, or overwhelmed.

Typical Fight Talk Behaviors

Demanding, ordering: "Do it like I say, and don't ask me why."

Blaming, accusing, attacking, scolding: "Why did you break it? And don't tell me you didn't. I saw you with my own eyes."

Threatening consequences: "Say that one more time and I'll leave."

Labeling: "You're lazy and irresponsible."

Name-calling, belittling, using loaded words: "Look at the way you're eating. You're a pig."

Defending: "My idea isn't so dumb. You're just jealous because you didn't come up with it."

Interrogating: "Tell me what you're thinking. You just sit there with that stupid smile and don't say anything."

Judging/putting down: "You never do it right! If you had a brain, you wouldn't know what to do with it."

Challenging/taunting: "Your mother's favorite son could never do anything wrong."

Lecturing/moralizing/preaching: "You shouldn't even let those thoughts enter your head."

Bragging: "When I was your age, I could work three times as hard as you."

Psychologizing, diagnosing: "I suggest you find the real cause of your defensiveness. You're paranoid."

Cursing/foul language

Impact of Fight Talk

In Fight Talk you are out of control, off balance, and out of touch with your self-awareness. You attack others and defend yourself. You say mean and hurtful things that you later regret. This distresses you, your partner, and your relationship.

The focus of Fight Talk is always on the other person, never on yourself. In your rush to get your partner to change, you overlook or avoid your own contribution and response to the situation. Furthermore, Fight Talk attacks the other person's worth or esteem, not just his or her behavior about an issue.

In Fight Talk, you fight fire with fire. You act out your surface feeling of anger rather than act on your underlying feelings of fear, hurt, or resentment.

While Fight Talk gets juices flowing and may break up a logjam once in awhile, its success is short-lived if it is used often. It does not promote positive long-term solutions to tough relationship issues. Instead, it can erupt in emotional and physical violence — abuse which destroys relationships.

Fight Talk says that you and your partner are not attending to a deeper issue. Use it as a cue to expand your own and the other person's awareness about the real issue. Ask yourself, "What's behind my Fight Talk? What do I fear?"

SPITE TALK

Spite Talk is angry and indirect, signaling hurt and resentment. People use these spiteful messages when they believe they have no ability to influence situations directly and positively.

Spite Talk exerts great power as "powerless," passive non-compliance. The threat or capacity to withdraw and sabotage can be very controlling. It is the ultimate in resistance.

Spite Talk tries to exert control from a "one down," rather than a "one up," position of power. It is an obtuse way to express helplessness and hopelessness. It attempts to spread guilt and shame.

Typical Spite Talk Behaviors

Shooting zingers, taking pot shots: "If you're so smart, you do it."

Implying poor me — ain't it awful: "Nobody ever asks me if I want to go."

Nagging: "Do I always have to remind you to take off your shoes when you come in?"

Foot-dragging: "I know I said I'd do it. When I have time, I'll get around to it."

Complaining, whining: "How come I always have to do the dirty work?"

Pouting/ignoring/withholding affection (going about business in silent unresponsiveness)

Withholding information: "I told you once. If you don't remember what I said, I'm not going to repeat it."

Withdrawing angrily: "It's not my problem. What do I care?"

Denying: "No, nothing's wrong. What makes you think that?"

Cynicism/sarcasm: "Well, look who's graced us with her presence."

Placating: "No, that's all right. Let's do it your way. I'm sure it will come out better."

Being a martyr or victim (covering for others, accepting blame): "It was probably my fault again. I should have . . . ."

Putting self down: "If I wasn't so dumb, I would have caught the mistake."

Gossiping/being self-righteous: "I would never think of stooping that low."

Keeping score/reprisals: "I won't forget what you just said."

Lying/distorting: "I called Jack yesterday (no call was made)."

Attempt to guilt other: "You know you'll be wrong if you do that."

Impact of Spite Talk

Spite Talk communicates a "poor me" attitude. It can represent a long-term, mindstyle/lifestyle of low self-esteem, or more commonly, it is a temporary response to a particular situation. Spite Talk can continue a conflict under the surface. In any event, using or hearing Spite Talk is very draining. Energy and information are dissipated rather than channeled into productive change.

In the long run, people who use Spite Talk hurt themselves most by misusing their own power.

REACTIVE LISTENING

In Reactive Listening, controlling is more important than connecting. You are closed to your partner's genuine awareness. You listen long enough to formulate a reaction to what the talker is saying, and then you interrupt and counter with your own perspective. In the process, you attempt to take the lead away from the person talking by taking control of the conversation and getting him or her to agree to and comply with your counter response.

As your partner talks, you are active internally and externally, reacting to what is being said. Rather than taking in and digesting information, in a split second, you:

- Evaluate fragments (right, wrong, good, bad, true, untrue)

- Rehearse your next speech

- Attempt to take over

From a positive standpoint, your reaction may be an efficient attempt to dissuade, persuade, or even reassure the talker. In certain situations, your ability to take charge with minimal information can be helpful.

However, on the negative side, you may listen only to gain ammunition for shooting down your partner's point of view and defending your own. Reactive Listening often ignores, twists, distorts, or manipulates what the other person says in an attempt to force agreement. The listener gathers information for intimidation and retaliation.

Typical Reactive Listening Behaviors

Short attention span

Frequent interruptions

Fixed eye contact (possibly hard)

Upper-body tension

Negative tone

Active/direct aggressive or agitated gestures
    (physical crowding)

Passive/indirect, disengaging gestures
    (physical distancing)

Closed/leading questions

"Why" questions

Mind reading

Internal judging and rehearsing

Frequent completion of other's sentences

Impact of Reactive Listening

As with Control Talk, Reactive Listening can be an efficient style. More often, however, the listener discounts the talker by attempting to take the floor away from him or her. The struggle for who talks and who listens accelerates — tension, defensiveness, and resistance grow. This spawns fragmented and inaccurate information. In the process of generating distorted and misleading information, bad feelings and misunderstandings develop.

While this style of listening may energize an exchange, it often results in a competitive, often mean, power struggle with no one feeling positive about the outcome and neither partner open to the other.

STYLE II COMMUNICATION

Intention to be:
in charge
helpful
persuasive
efficient

Mood/Nonverbals:
energized
authoritative

Intention to:
control/lead
direct
persuade
instruct
evaluate
set expectations/limits
positively reinforce
use legitimate authority
gain agreement/compliance
ignore

Control Talk
Reactive Listening

Fight Talk | Spite Talk

Intention to be:
right
justified
hurtful (sometimes)

Intention to:
force
attack
defend/counter
avoid responsibility
hide fear/vulnerability
intimidate
bluff
compete/win

Mood/Nonverbals:
tense
anxious
aggressive
hostile
abusive

Cue words:
you, we, it, they
"why" questions
statements phrased as questions
imperatives (should, ought, have to)
superlatives (always, never, every)
assumptions

Intention to be:
noticed
pitied
uncooperative
seen as helpless

Intention to:
manipulate
cover hurt
protect
thwart change
get even/retaliate
twist/distort

Mood/Nonverbals:
lethargic
resentful
indifferent
disengaged
defiant
cynical
hopeless
silently angry

Red Flags generally not good in relationships.

STYLE III

SEARCH TALK
EXPLORATIVE LISTENING

Search Talk and Explorative Listening revolve around non-routine matters or uncertain and complex issues that may be very fuzzy and undefined. They are cool, objective, and rational styles of communication for exploring facts and examining possibilities. The styles are good for "stepping back" and seeing a bigger picture — gaining an overview of the dynamics surrounding an issue.

SEARCH TALK

Search Talk has a tentative quality to it. You can use it to speculate about causes, pose solutions, and play out various scenarios without committing yourself to any particular direction. The time orientation in Search Talk is toward either the past or future, but not the present moment. It is a safe way to "test the water" by making observations or raising questions to get a handle on things.

Typical Search Talk Behaviors

Identifying issues: "I'm wondering if we are letting outside activities crowd our time together."

Giving relevant background information: "Between us we carry about twelve credit cards."

Analyzing causes: "Maybe you're so fatigued at the end of a day because you aren't getting enough exercise."

Giving impressions/explanations: "I think maybe we eat out too much."

Making interpretations: "Barb's phone call probably means she's convinced."

Brainstorming or generating possibilities: "Perhaps you could set a time to jog every other day. How about playing tennis together twice a week?"

Posing solutions: "Suppose you go back to school in the fall. How do you think that would work?"

Impact of Search Talk

Search Talk is very helpful for reducing pressure and increasing information. By probing for information in this non-accusatory fashion, you are free to identify and clarify issues and events, examine relevant background information, and generate alternative courses of action. In effect, Search Talk becomes a "think tank" to play out ideas and expand options for the future.

The nonthreatening, nonjudgmental nature of Search Talk gives both you and your partner chances to be heard. By itself, however, Search Talk usually only skims across the surface and misses the core of an issue. This leaves the issue unresolved and partners dissatisfied because crucial affective information does not surface.

Speculation, reflection, and exploration can turn into "float talk" — a sophisticated way to avoid resolving issues — where no one takes responsibility for putting insights into action. Search Talk works best in combination with the next talking style, Straight Talk, to get to the heart of issues and take action.

EXPLORATIVE LISTENING

Explorative Listening searches for significant information surrounding complex or nonroutine issues. In this style, you ask open questions to gain background information — data and ideas about what has really caused an event to occur — as well as thoughts about how to solve problems.

When you listen exploratively, you are truly interested in hearing what you partner thinks about an issue. In this search mode, you want to gain perspective, expand knowledge, clarify misunderstandings, and clear up confusion.

Typical Explorative Listening Behaviors:

Increased attending

Receptive body posture

Intermittent eye contact

Open questions

Impact of Explorative Listening

Explorative Listening takes the pressure off the moment by opening the discussion. Using open questions, which is typical of this style, has the effect of increasing the quality of information over Conventional or Reactive styles of listening.

The open questions can be helpful for focusing the discussion when someone talks long and broadly about a topic. Open questions can also stimulate conversation when someone generally has little to say.

Explorative Listening has its limitations, however. First, many people have a tendency to focus their questions on data, thoughts, and actions. They overlook feelings and wants. This gives the discussion a cautious, non-affective quality. Secondly, open questions can structure an exchange. Inadvertently, the listener, with the questions he or she asks, can take control of the conversation if the talker chooses to answer those questions. The questions, rather than keeping the discussion open, begin to narrow the interaction.

STYLE III COMMUNICATION

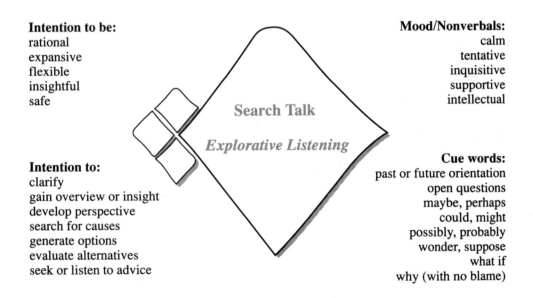

Intention to be:
rational
expansive
flexible
insightful
safe

Mood/Nonverbals:
calm
tentative
inquisitive
supportive
intellectual

Search Talk

Explorative Listening

Intention to:
clarify
gain overview or insight
develop perspective
search for causes
generate options
evaluate alternatives
seek or listen to advice

Cue words:
past or future orientation
open questions
maybe, perhaps
could, might
possibly, probably
wonder, suppose
what if
why (with no blame)

STYLE IV

STRAIGHT TALK
ATTENTIVE LISTENING

Straight Talk and Attentive Listening begin where the other styles never venture. In this style, you go to the heart of an issue by using the six talking skills to disclose self-information left unsaid in other styles — particularly feelings and wants.

Likewise, to tune into the other person, you use listening skills. The goal of this style is to *connect* with yourself and the other person. Your aim is to build, not to destroy. You do this by *managing yourself* rather than by *manipulating others*.

STRAIGHT TALK

Straight Talk builds on full awareness, both your own and your partner's. You orient yourself, timewise, to the present moment. In the process, you deal *completely* and *congruently* with tension and differences without blaming, demanding, defending, or deceiving. Straight Talk supports you and your partner to work through issues productively — generating collaborative action plans that fit for both people.

Develop The 10
Commandments
of straight talk

In Straight Talk, you:

- *Acknowledge* your own and your partner's awareness — your sensory data, thoughts, feelings, wants, and actions.

- *Accept* what you find as "what is," rather than disregarding, denying, or running from it.

- *Act* on, not react to, this awareness.

In Straight Talk you use all the talking skills to communicate your awareness: speak for self; describe sensory data; express thoughts; share feelings; disclose wants; and state actions.

Typical Straight Talk Behaviors

Focusing on the issue: "Here's how I see what's going on."

Identifying tension: "I'm feeling very frustrated right now."

Acknowledging differences: "Well, I think we differ on this. You want to go to school full time next year, and I think just part time would be better."

Requesting feedback: "Have you noticed, after I ask Matt for his ideas, whether I do something that shuts him off when he begins to speak?"

Giving feedback: "I've noticed that when you speak, you drop your voice at the end of sentences and it's difficult for me to hear you."

Expressing appreciation: "Thank you for backing me up in our discussion with the kids. Your support gave me confidence to hang in there on this tough decision."

Revealing impact: "When you said my idea wasn't important, that hurt me."

Sharing vulnerability: "Basically, I don't feel as confident as I let on."

Asking for change: "When I'm talking on the phone, I would like not to be interrupted. Would you agree to this?"

Taking responsibility for your own contribution/response: "Yeah, I didn't listen to you. I assumed that I knew what you felt, so I started thinking about what to do next instead of listening."

Apologizing/asking for forgiveness: "I really did hurt you by leaving you out. I'm sorry I did that. I want to apologize and assure you that I will not do that again."

Giving support: "I will back up your decision."

Impact of Straight Talk

Straight Talk is a nonabrasive, powerful style if you are not trying to be powerful — controlling. (As soon as you use Straight Talk to be powerful, you will slip into a control mode and lose power.) In Straight Talk you can feel peaceful even though you are discussing a difficult matter if your intentions are to connect and collaborate rather than to control and manipulate.

In Straight Talk, you can be tough yet tender, firm yet flexible, and caring but not controlling. The real power of the style comes from putting your cards on the table without playing tricks, pushing, or shoving. As you disclose your awareness and seek the same from your partner, each of you is recognized as an authority on your own experience.

There is a risk in Straight Talk. As you disclose more about yourself, you increase the listener's choices. The information you supply can be used constructively or destructively, moving you closer together or pushing you further apart. You can become vulnerable. Usually disclosure begets disclosure and results in new understanding, acceptance, and intimacy between you and your partner. However, Straight Talk does not always move you closer to one another. Sometimes relationships are severed when people are straight with each other.

The results of most Straight Talk conversations are positive. As partners share their real thoughts and feelings about issues without experiencing reprisals, real trust grows. You leave conversations with good feelings about yourself and your partner because each of you understands the other's viewpoint, and both of you recognize that each of you has been understood.

Be cautioned: Do not try to use Straight Talk to pretend that you have a caring attitude or are being collaborative, if neither is true. The other person will see and hear your incongruent nonverbals signaling your desire to control and will distrust you. If your intention is to be in control (which is the behavior of Style II), say so. Your disclosure of that intention is using the Straight Talk style, which gives the other person the choice to go along with you or not.

Straight Talk has its limits. It is not a "cure all" or "quick fix." It does not guarantee you will get your way. It demonstrates commitment to an open process.

ATTENTIVE LISTENING

One of the quickest ways to connect with someone when there is an issue present is to listen attentively to him or her — letting that person express his or her awareness — wherever that leads you. When you attentively listen, you do not rehearse, evaluate, or redirect. Rather, you put your concerns aside temporarily and simply follow what the other is saying — trying to be in his or her shoes. This is the surest way to reduce interpersonal tension, establish rapport, and build trust.

As you attentively listen to your partner, you show care and respect for him or her as you seek to discover and understand what he or she is experiencing.

Attentive Listening revolves primarily around four of the five listening skills in the Listening Cycle: attending — looking, listening, tracking; acknowledging the other's experience; inviting more information; and summarizing to ensure accuracy. (The skill of asking open questions typically occurs with Explorative Listening, Style III communication.)

Typical Attentive Listening Behaviors:

Soft and sustained eye contact

Calm and responsive body posture

Attending behavior

Acknowledging responses

Inviting comments and questions

Summarizing messages

Impact of Attentive Listening

Using the listening skills to discover and understand your partner's awareness (even though you may not necessarily agree with what you hear) creates a complete and accurate information base. Plus, your partner's esteem is enhanced in the process. In turn, attentively listening to your partner earns you the chance to be heard and understood if the issue involves a two-way exchange.

STYLE IV COMMUNICATION

Intention to be:
open
clear
understanding
direct
accurate
responsible
truthful
assertive
responsive
respectful
tactful

Intention to:
disclose
attune/follow
act on "what is"
connect, not control
count self and other
care
collaborate

Straight Talk

Attentive Listening

Mood/Nonverbals:
attentive
involved
serious
centered
focused

Cue words:
"I" pronouns
feeling words
want comments

now orientation
will (future action)

Disclosure and Receptivity

When you take steps into the Search-Talk and Straight-Talk territories as described on the Communication Styles Map, you progressively increase your *self-disclosure* to your partner. And, when you enter the Explorative- or Attentive-Listening areas, you heighten your *receptivity* to what he or she has to say. Using the talking and listening skills can bring you into these styles. As a result of being in these styles, you and your partner experience deeper empathy, trust, and understanding between you.

MIXED MESSAGES

Mixed messages occur when any controlling intention or behavior from Style II slips into another style. One part of the message is Style I, III, or IV, but a second Style-II part adds an undercurrent that usually contradicts the original style.

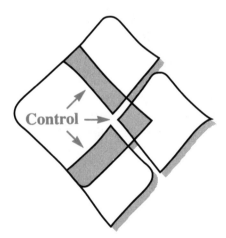

Mixed messages create confusion and are hard to deal with because receivers do not know whether to respond to the control part or the other style. Mixed messages also spawn caution and resistance. If the Style-II part includes elements of Fight Talk or Spite Talk, the receiver usually just hears the negative element.

While some mixed messages can be playful and fun, they are tricky. For example, if someone mixes Small Talk with Fight Talk and says to you, "You're pretty smart for such a dumb guy," what is the message? Is it a compliment or a put down? If you take it as a compliment, you might be naive. If you take it as a put down, the other person might deny that was the intention and say, "What's wrong, can't you take a joke?"

Most mixed messages grow out of incongruence — saying one thing but feeling another — or an undercurrent of unresolved issues. They take several forms:

- *Presumptions about the other person:* "I'd tell you about my day if you were really interested."

- *But or yes, but:* "I agree with what you're saying, but it still isn't a good idea."

- *Offer/condition:* "I'll treat you nicely when you start treating me nicely."

- *Build up, put down (positive-negative):* "You really did a thorough job on your report, but it sure took you long enough."

A variety of behavioral cues signals mixed messages. They include vocal characteristics, such as a harsh voice or a whiny, sarcastic, or demanding tone and facial expressions that do not match the idea expressed, such as a smile or grin with a complaint. As you talk and listen, be aware of these nonverbal messages.

The most effective way to respond to a mixed message is to acknowledge both parts and ask for clarification about the clear style and the undercurrent: the statement and the presumption; the yes and the but; the offer and the condition; the build up and the put down. Then ask the sender which part he or she means most.

As a sender, if you find yourself slipping into mixed messages when you do not want to, look at your wants and feelings and express them in Straight Talk.

CONFLICT RESOLUTION AND STYLES OF COMMUNICATION

Recall from Chapter 3 that in dealing with issues, people use any of the following processes: avoid; persuade (including fight or capitulate); float; compromise; or collaborate. These processes, as well as the resulting outcomes, are intricately linked with the styles of communication. By using a particular talking and listening style, when discussing an issue, you determine your conflict resolution process.

CONFLICT RESOLUTION	**STYLES OF COMMUNICATION**
Processes:	Styles:
• Avoid	• Small/Shop Talk
	Conventional Listening
• Persuade	• Control Talk
Fight/Capitulate	Fight/Spite
	Reactive Listening
• Float	• Search Talk
	Explorative Listening
• Compromise	
• Collaborate	• Straight Talk
	Attentive Listening

By staying in Style I, you tend to avoid an issue. Or, through talking and listening in Style II, you attempt to persuade. If you do only Search Talk and Explorative Listening, you are likely to float. Adding some Style IV to Style III, you can compromise. Finally, if you use Straight Talk and Attentive Listening (along with Style III as you do in the Mapping-an-Issue structure, for instance), you can collaborate to reach an outcome.

Being aware of your style can give you choice about the process you employ in dealing with an issue. By consciously shifting your style, you can change the process. You can be proactive rather than passive or reactive, and you can use a positive approach rather than a negative one.

Use All of the Styles

No one style handles all situations. Each style serves a special purpose and communicates something different. The key is flexibility — being able to match style and situation appropriately instead of getting stuck in just one style. For example, using Straight Talk in a social setting may be out of place and make others uncomfortable. Yet in a situation where an issue is at hand, you can quickly head off a potential argument by using Straight Talk and Attentive Listening.

The choice of a communication style to use is yours. In making your choice, pay attention to your attitude — how you care about yourself and your partner.

COMMUNICATION-STYLES OBSERVATION

Instructions: Use the space below to jot down key words and phrases you hear (for feedback later) that indicate a particular style of communication. Also note nonverbal behaviors associated with the style.

	Partner #1	Partner #2
I Small Talk		
Shop Talk		
Conventional		
II Control Talk		
Fight Talk		
Spite Talk		
Reactive		
III Search Talk		
Explorative		
IV Straight Talk		
Attentive		

COMMUNICATION STYLES ACTION PLAN

Instructions: Think of the styles of communication you and your partner use when the two of you are conversing together. Estimate the percentage of time each of you *currently* spends in each talking and listening style.

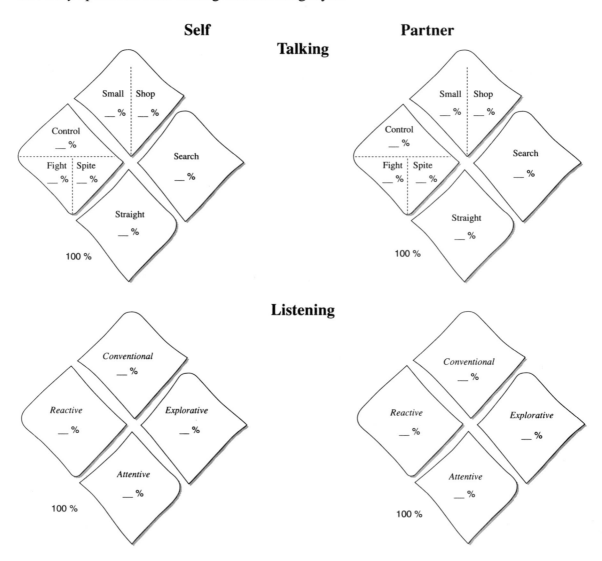

1. Compare and discuss, with your partner, the styles and percentages you have identified with those he or she has identified.

2. Choose styles for yourself to increase and decrease.

OBSERVING/COACHING A DISCUSSION OF AN ISSUE IN STYLES III AND IV

To Observe:

- Look for:

  Style III, Search Talk and Explorative Listening — tentative, speculative, and explorative communication, using open questions and expressions of thoughts

  Style IV, Straight Talk and Attentive Listening — clear, direct, and focused communication which includes explicit disclosure of feelings and wants, using combinations of the talking skills and the listening skills

To Coach:

- If you think the conversation could benefit from brainstorming, speculation, or clarifying information, encourage the use of open questions and thought statements.

- If you think the exchange could benefit from deepening or focusing, encourage disclosure of sensory data, feelings, wants, and actions as well as use of the listening skills: acknowledge, invite, and summarize.

OBSERVING PARTNERS' DISCUSSION OF AN ISSUE IN STYLES III AND IV

Here are the talking and listening skills taught in Couple Communication I:

Talking Skills
Speak for Self
Describe *Sensory Data*
Express *Thoughts*
Share *Feelings*
Disclose *Wants*
State *Actions*

Listening Skills
Attend, Look, Listen, Track
Acknowledge Other's Experience
Invite More Information
Summarize To Ensure Accuracy
Ask Open Questions

Instructions: Follow the talking and listening skills of one partner. In the space below, note key words or phrases (for feedback later) that demonstrate clear use of skills. Also note which skills demonstrate which styles (III or IV).

Talking Skills   **Listening Skills**

CHANGE FIGHT AND SPITE TALK TO STRAIGHT TALK

Each of the ten statements below is an example of Fight Talk or Spite Talk. Use the space between statements to change the message into Straight Talk and Search Talk.

1. "You never help around here, and I do it all. You're lazy."

2. "You're always late. Can't you ever be on time?"

3. "Don't be a jerk. Grow up."

4. "We'll just do what you say, since you're always right" (sarcastic tone).

5. "If I was as smart as you, I would have seen the mistake."

6. "You're too quiet in social situations. You look dumb."

7. "No, nothing's wrong. What makes you think that?"

8. "Nobody ever pays attention to me."

9. "You're selfish and inconsiderate."

Some possible Straight Talk statements for the sentences above include the following:

1. "I feel overwhelmed with so many chores, and I'd like some help. Would you be willing to help me?"

2. "I get frustrated and angry when you don't arrive at the time we agreed upon."

3. "Here's what I'd like to see, because I think it shows more responsibility."

4. "I don't agree with how you want us to do this. Can we talk about an alternative?"

5. "I didn't see the mistake."

6. "I feel uncomfortable when I think you're too quiet in social situations."

7. "Yes, I am upset. I think I'm being discounted."

8. "I wish we could talk together now."

9. "I think you mainly think about yourself and don't consider others. For instance, . . ."

TALKING STYLES WITH KIDS OR CO-WORKERS

Instructions: Think of various situations in the past when you were with a child, adolescent, or co-worker. You used one of the talking styles listed below, and then felt uncomfortable about the conversation. What was your intention in each situation? What was the resulting mood and outcome?

Past Situation (or Issue)

Small Talk or Shop Talk

Control Talk

Fight Talk

Spite Talk

Search Talk

Straight Talk

Now anticipate a smilar situation with the same person. Plan how you can use the styles appropriately. (Rehearse some cue words, behaviors, or skills.)

Future Situation (or Issue)

Small Talk or Shop Talk

Control Talk

Search Talk

Straight Talk

EXPRESSING APPRECIATION IN STRAIGHT TALK

Instructions: Think of something for which you would like to give your partner thanks. Use the Awareness Wheel below to organize a Straight Talk message.

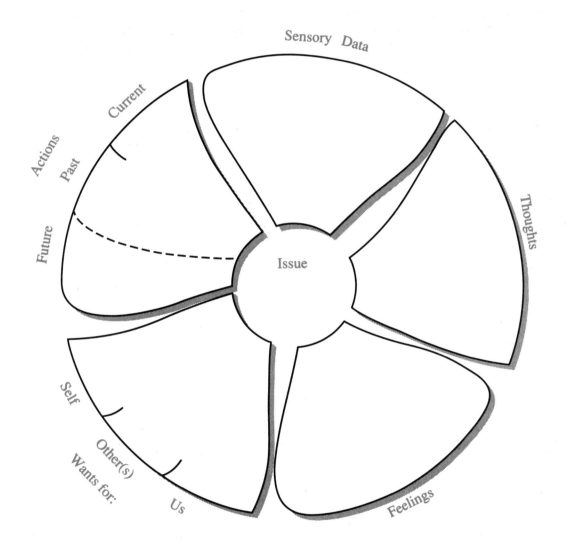

Pick an appropriate time and place to share your appreciation.

POST-QUESTIONNAIRE

Date _____

Here are questions relating to the concepts and skills taught in Couple Communication I.

Instructions: Without reviewing how you marked your Pre-Questionnaire, follow the four steps below to assess how you are currently communicating with your partner, and to determine how well you have achieved your learning goals.

Step 1. Mark each item twice: first with an "X" to represent your *typical* behavior and again with an "O" (circle) to represent your more-so or less-so *desired* behavior. If your *typical* and *desired* behaviors are the same, the "X" and "O" marks will be on the same number. If they are not the same, the marks will fall on different numbers.

When you are with your partner, how often do you:

	Seldom Often	Difference
1. Speak for your partner — put words into his or her mouth?	1 2 3 4 5 6	_____
2. Use your full awareness to reflect on an issue?	1 2 3 4 5 6	_____
3. Share your feelings?	1 2 3 4 5 6	_____
4. Disclose your wants and desires?	1 2 3 4 5 6	_____
5. Listen briefly, then begin talking?	1 2 3 4 5 6	_____
6. Acknowledge what your partner is feeling?	1 2 3 4 5 6	_____
7. Acknowledge your partner's wants and desires?	1 2 3 4 5 6	_____
8. Invite/encourage your partner to expand on his or her point?	1 2 3 4 5 6	_____
9. Ask what he or she is thinking, feeling, and wanting?	1 2 3 4 5 6	_____
10. Summarize your partner's messages to ensure accuracy?	1 2 3 4 5 6	_____
11. Avoid issues?	1 2 3 4 5 6	_____
12. Propose a good time and place to discuss important issues?	1 2 3 4 5 6	_____

	Seldom	Often	Difference
13. Force decisions on your partner?	1 2 3 4 5 6		_____
14. Give in to your partner's decisions?	1 2 3 4 5 6		_____
15. Talk about issues but leave them unresolved?	1 2 3 4 5 6		_____
16. Settle issues by compromising — trading something for something?	1 2 3 4 5 6		_____
17. Resolve issues by building agreements collaboratively?	1 2 3 4 5 6		_____
18. Have pleasant, fun conversations?	1 2 3 4 5 6		_____
19. Direct or instruct your partner?	1 2 3 4 5 6		_____
20. Argue and fight?	1 2 3 4 5 6		_____
21. Blame or attack him or her directly?	1 2 3 4 5 6		_____
22. Make spiteful, undercutting remarks indirectly?	1 2 3 4 5 6		_____
23. Explore possible causes of an issue?	1 2 3 4 5 6		_____
24. Brainstorm solutions to an issue?	1 2 3 4 5 6		_____
25. Send clear, complete, and straightforward messages?	1 2 3 4 5 6		_____
Total Difference Score			_____

Step 2. When you have completed marking all the items, calculate the numerical difference between *typical* and *desired* scores for each item and record the results in the "difference" column. If the "X" and "O" are on the same number, the difference = 0. If the "X" is on 5 and the "O" is on 2, the difference = 3. Note that the "O" can be located on a higher or lower number than the "X." Do not be concerned about the higher or lower direction of the scores, just calculate the numerical difference between the marks.

Step 3. Sum the difference scores. (See the next page to review your skill learning.)

REVIEW YOUR SKILL LEARNING

When you have completed scoring your Post-Questionnaire, turn to your Pre-Questionnaire located in the Introduction to *Talking and Listening Together.* Consider the following:

1. Determine how well you have achieved the learning goals you set for yourself on the Pre-Questionnaire.

2. Compare any changes in the "Total Difference Scores" from Pre- to Post-Questionnaires.

   A lower score (from Pre- to Post- Questionnaire) indicates that you have progressed closer to your *desired* skill use.

   A higher score (from Pre- to Post- Questionnaire) indicates that you have moved further away from your *desired* skill use.*

3. Share your accomplishments with your partner.**

---

*   If you have an increase in your Post-Questionnaire Difference Score, here are two reasons this can happen. (1) You might be using more skills now, yet you also realize how much more effectively you could use the skills. (2) You might not have achieved the skill-learning progress you desired. If this is true, you may wish to consult with your Couple Communication I instructor about your results.

** For Your Information: In the Pre- and Post- Questionnaires, items 1 – 4 relate to Chapter 1, the Awareness Wheel and talking skills; items 5 – 10 capture Chapter 2, listening skills; items 11 – 17 relate to conflict resolution and Mapping Issues; items 18 – 25 represent the styles of communication.

ABOUT THE AUTHORS

Sherod Miller, Ph.D., is President of Interpersonal Communication Programs, Inc., a publishing and consulting firm. Dr. Miller specializes in interpersonal communication skill training and team building for new work systems. He has worked with numerous corporations, government agencies, and human service organizations. He is co-author of *Working Together: Productive Communication on the Job.* He is a Fellow in the American Association of Marriage and Family Therapists, and was formerly a faculty member in the Department of Medicine at the University of Minnesota, School of Medicine.

Phyllis A. Miller, Ph.D., is Vice-President of Interpersonal Communication Programs, Inc. She is also an independent consultant to corporations and government organizations, specializing in business writing and speed/efficient reading. She is the author of *Managing Your Reading* and the audio cassette program, *Productive Reading.* She also wrote and presented *Flexible Reading,* a video course that airs on public television and in businesses and schools. Together with her husband, Sherod Miller, she teaches Couple Communication programs.

Elam W. Nunnally, Ph.D., is Associate Professor of Social Welfare at the University of Wisconsin-Milwaukee. He is a marriage and family therapist specializing in communication and in brief therapy, which he teaches in Scandinavia and in the U.S. He has also co-authored the five-volume series on *Families in Trouble* as well as *Communication Basics for Human Services Professionals,* Sage Publications.

Daniel B. Wackman, Ph. D., is Director of the School of Journalism and Mass Communication at the University of Minnesota. Much of his research has focused on family processes. He also serves as a consultant to business, nonprofit organizations, and government agencies. His most recent book is *Managing Media Organizations: Effective Leadership of the Media.*

The authors also collaborated to write *Connecting With Self and Others* and the *Connecting Skills Workbook,* published by Interpersonal Communication Programs, Inc.

OTHER RESOURCES

Prepare: for Engaged Couples
Enrich: for Married Couples

Prepare and Enrich are two tools we recommend for systematically assessing your issues as a couple. The instruments provide feedback on strengths and work areas in your relationship.

To take either instrument, you and your partner each complete a questionnaire that is then computer scored. You receive feedback in the following areas: leisure activities, realistic expectations (in Prepare only), marital satisfaction (in Enrich only), personality issues, communication, conflict, family and friends, children and parenting, equalitarian roles, religious orientation, financial management, sexual relationship, cohesion and adaptability.

For more information on Prepare or Enrich, contact:

Prepare/Enrich, Inc.
P. O. Box 109
Minneapolis, MN 55458
1-800-331-1661

The Association for Couples in Marriage Enrichment

ACME is an international organization committed to helping couples develop the skills needed to improve their relationships. The Association provides retreats, workshops, learning events, and resources for couples.

For the name and address of an ACME contact person in your area, write or call:

ACME
459 South Church Street
P.O. Box 10596
Winston-Salem, North Carolina 27108
1-800-634-8325

ALSO AVAILABLE FROM ICP, INC.

COLLABORATIVE TEAM SKILLS

This program teaches groups who work together to use the frameworks, skills, and processes that COUPLE COMMUNICATION (CC) teaches couples. As in CC, participants in COLLABORATIVE TEAM SKILLS use real issues (not roleplays) as they learn how to communicate about situations and resolve conflicts more effectively.

COLLABORATIVE TEAM SKILLS is useful in the following contexts:
- Team Building
- Staff Development
- Implementation of Self-Directed Work Teams
- Group Tune-Up/Re-Alignment

For more information, contact ICP.

For a catalog about all ICP programs, materials, and training, contact:

Interpersonal Communication Programs, Inc.
7201 So. Broadway, Suite 11
Littleton, Colorado 80122
303-794-1764   Fax 303-798-3392
800-328-5099